MW01167019

POEMS
of
PRAISE
and
MORE

POEMS
of
PRAISE
and
MORE

HUSTER H.

TATE PUBLISHING
AND ENTERPRISES, LLC

Published by Tate Publishing & Enterprises, LLC
127 E. Trade Center Terrace | Mustang, Oklahoma 73064 USA
1.888.361.9473 | www.tatepublishing.com

Tate Publishing is committed to excellence in the publishing industry. The company reflects the philosophy established by the founders, based on Psalm 68:11,
"The Lord gave the word and great was the company of those who published it."

Book design copyright © 2013 by Tate Publishing, LLC. All rights reserved.
Cover design by Rtor Maghuyop
Interior design by Mary Jean Archival

Published in the United States of America

ISBN: 978-1-62902-891-0
1. Poetry / Subjects & Themes / Inspirational & Religious
2. Religion / Christian Life / Inspirational
13.11.18

Contents

The Beginning

This is the beginning of a book of poems you see,
of which God did write for many of you and for me.

God did write it for you and for me you see.
God did write it to give us a better way to be.

Satan tried everything in his power to stop this book,
however, there is just one thing that he overlooked,

and that is that God is the author of it and not me.
God gave it to me and I gave it to Satan you see.

Then Satan messed it up and gave it back to me.
It took me years to straighten it out, but you see

I gave it to Satan because I did not care.
Now it is back together and now I do care.

If it changes one life, it will be worth it.
Well, here it is and I hope you enjoy it.

What a Friend and More Christ Is

I

My life was a mess.
Life was hell I confess.
And throughout my life I needed help.

I was lost in sin.
I did not care then.
And he found me when I needed help.

See, he found me when
my sins numbered in tens.
And I was glad that I had some help.

Although my sins were many.
Even though my sins were plenty.
He forgave me my sins and he did help.

God and Jesus saved my soul
and then Jesus made me whole.
And on Christ I am sincerely sold.

What a Friend and More he is.
What a Friend and More Christ is.
And at the right hand of God Jesus is.

He is the Son of God and Son of man.
He is the Word of God and Hope of man.
He is the Lamb of God and Light of man.

"He is the King of kings and Lord of lords."
"He is the Prince of peace and Prince of life."
"He is the bread of life and the water of life."

"He is the resurrection and the life."
"He is the way, the truth and the life."
"He is the way we are to be and the life."

He is the life with nail-scarred hands,
who died for the sins of men & women.
and we do need you, Jesus Christ. Amen.

What a Friend and More Christ Is

II

My life was a mess.
Life was hell I confess.
And throughout my wretched life I did need help.

I was not aware when
I did need some help then.
And an angel made me aware that I did need help.

I was told the way of help.
I did stray from the way for help.
And I did wander off on my own lost way for help.

I was in need of help.
I did not plead for help.
And I had no clue as to who to turn to for help.

I was guilty as sin.
I could not win then.
And I did not see any real way for help.

I was sick from sin.
I was not well then.
And I did not know who to look to for help.

I was dying from my sin,
when he did talk to me then.
And I did ask him who to look to for help.

I was well aware of my sin,
when he did talk to me again then.
And I did hear who to look to for help.

I was a slave of sin.
I did need freedom then.
And I did take the angel's advice for help.

I was lost in sin.
I did not care then.
And I did look to the Saviour for help.

Then he found me when
my sins numbered in tens.
And I did rejoice when I had some help.

My sins they were many.
My sins they were plenty.
And he did make me see and he did help.

He did forgive me of my sin
and then he did immediately begin
to set my soul completely free from my sin.

He did set my soul free
and then he made me see
the way we are supposed to be.

He did care for me then
and then he did love me when
my wretched soul was in slavery to sin.

He did make me care
and then I was aware
Jesus really was there.

He did take me in
and then I cared again,
because he gave me hope then.

He did give me life anew
and then he took away my strife, too,
and I do look forward to the day when I do say I do.

He did help save my soul
and then he made me whole.
And on Christ, I am totally sold.

He is a Friend and More he is.
What a Friend and More Christ is.
And at the right hand of God Jesus is.

He is bravo.
He is mucho gusto.
He is not macho or machismo.

He is with it.
He is terrific,
to be specific.

He is a caretaker.
He is no care actor.
And he has character.

He is a card.
He tried very hard.
and he was marred and scarred.

He was marred and scarred by men.
His purpose on the cross was for men.
And we do need you Sweet Jesus. Amen.

What a Friend and More Christ Is

III

My life was a mess.
Life was hell I confess.
And throughout my wretched life I needed help.

I was in a whirl.
I chased the girls.
And there was no one in the world for to help.

I was not in the world
and I was of the world.
And I needed the Saviour of the world to help.

I was nearly insane
from the mental strain.
And I did think that I was way beyond help.

I was heartbroken
and he was soft-spoken.
And Christ Jesus asked if I needed some help.

I was lost in sin.
I did not care then.
And I turned to the Sinless Saviour for help.

Then he found me when
my sins did number in tens.
And I was mad and glad that I had some help.

God and Christ saved my soul
and then Jesus made me whole.
And on them I am clearly sold.

He is a Friend and More he is.
What a Friend and More Christ is.
And at the right hand of God Jesus is.

He is kinder than kind.
He is easy on the mind.
He is better than a mine.

He is better than just smart.
He is gentle on the heart.
He is a brand-new start.

He has eyes like fire.
He has never been a liar.
He has earned the title of Sire.

He is bright eyed and bushy tailed.
His love for us will never fail.
He sees us through hell.

He will save us from the hell of life.
He will take us from dull to sharp knife.
He will rescue us from troubles and strife.

He loves us.
He needs us.
He earned us.

We love him.
We need him.
We adore him.

He's always there
no matter where,
when I need him.

He is always there
and he does care,
when I need him.

He is always there for men and women
and he died in lieu of men and women.
And we all do need you Jesus. Amen.

What a Friend and More Christ Is

IV

My life was a mess.
Life was hell I confess.
And throughout my life I did need help.

I was near my end
and he did help me then.
And throughout my life he did help.

He was near my friend
and he did hear my friend,
when I did call out to him for help.

I was guilty as sin
and he did forgive me my sin.
And he did answer my request for help.

I was a slave of sin
and he did free me from sin.
And I was glad that I had some help.

God and Christ saved my soul
and then Christ made me whole.
And on them I am decisively sold.

He is a Friend and More he is.
What a Friend and More Christ is.
And at the right hand of God Jesus is.

He is awesome.
Of him I am in awe of.
And on Jesus I am awestruck.

He is moonshine.
Of him I am moon-eyed.
And on Jesus I am moonstruck.

He is a jack of all trades
and a Master of all trades.
And you Christ will not trade.

He is there when you stray
and have gone your own way.
And you he will not ever betray.

He will stick with you through thick and thin.
He will forgive you all of all your sin.
And we do need you. Amen.

What a Friend and More Christ Is

V

I did not care then.
I was not aware when
I was without hope and was beyond help.

My life was a mess.
Life was hell I confess.
And I thought my life was beyond help.

I had lost my nerve.
Life I did not deserve.
And my life was lacking in moral help.

I had lost my mind.
I was not gentle or kind.
And my life was full of immoral help.

I had lost my will to live.
I had nothing left to give.
And I could not find any mortal help.

I had lost my soul.
I was far from whole.
And I searched for some immortal help.

I was lost in sin.
I needed help then.
And I asked for the Saviour for help.

Then he found me when
my sins numbered in tens.
And he did answer my request for help.
`
I was sick from sin.
I was not well then.
And Jesus Christ he did take me in.

He took me in
and then he did begin
to set my soul free from my sin.

God and Christ saved my soul
and then Christ made me whole.
And on them I am completely sold.

He is a Friend and More he is.
What a Friend and More Christ is.
And at the right hand of God Jesus is.

"He is the Saviour of the world."
"He is the Messiah of the world."
"He is the Redeemer of the world."

"He is the King of kings and Lord of lords."
"He is the Prince of peace and Prince of life."
"He is the bread of life and the water of life."

"He is the resurrection and the life."
"He is the way, the truth, and the life."
"He is the way we are to be and the life."

"He is the true way."
"He is the true vine."
"He is the true Light."

He is always true blue.
He is a dream come true.
He is Faithful and true.

"He is our faith, our hope, and our happiness."
"He is our Rock, our refuge, our forgiveness."
"He is THE Lord OUR RIGHTEOUSNESS."

"He is greater than the prince of darkness."
"He is the High Priest of the Most High God."
"He is the Shepherd and Bishop of our souls."

"He is the great shepherd of the sheep."
"He is the door of the sheep."
"He is the good shepherd."

"He is the root and the offspring of David."
"He is the Lion of the tribe of Judah."
"He is the bright and morning star."

"He is the Alpha and Omega."
"He is the First and the Last."
"He is the beginning and the end."

"He is the author and finisher of our faith."
"He is the author of eternal salvation
unto all them that obey him."

"He is to the right of The Most.
"He is next to The Lord of hosts.
"He is filled with The Holy Ghost.

He is always there for you all.
He is aware and cares for you all
and Jesus will swear too for you all.

He is always around.
He is never ever a clown
and he will not put you down.

He is always strong.
He is never ever wrong
and to him we all do belong.

He is a must.
He is never a bust
and in him we all do trust.

He is trustworthy.
He is praiseworthy
and he is noteworthy.

He is the Cream of the crop.
He is next to where the buck does stop
and Jesus is more than able to help you all a lot.

He is the Best of the best.
He is Master of all his tests
and he is better than the rest.

He is perfectly perfect.
He is especially Special
and he is honestly honest.

He is loving and caring.
He is austere and sincere
and Jesus is tender and mild.

He is gentle and humble.
He is more than ample
and he is an example.

He is a world shaker.
He is no heartbreaker
and he is a soul maker.

He is wondrous.
He is wonderful.
He is a wonder.

He is marvelous.
He is miraculous.
He is a mighty One.

He is considerate.
He is compassionate
and he is One of a kind.

He is kind.
He is kinder than kind
and Jesus is with God of One mind.

He is wise.
He is to us first prize
and he is the One who never lies.

He is cool.
He is never a fool
and he is the One who rules.

He is brave.
He is totally the rave
and he is the One who can save.

He is the One you are for my friend.
He is the One for you my friend
and he is for you my friend.

He is the anointed One.
He is the holy One.
He is the One.

He is One in a million.
He is One in a billion.
He is One in a trillion.

He is second only to God.
He is One with God.
He is with God.

He is our counselor with God.
He is our mediator with God.
He is our intercessor with God.

He is the love of God to man.
He is the life of God to man.
He is the gift of God to man.

He is the grace of God to man.
He is the mercy of God to man.
He is the peace of God to man.

He is the good will of God to man.
He is the salvation of God to man.
He is the redemption of God to man.

"He is the Son of God and Son of man."
"He is the Word of God and Hope of man."
"He is the Lamb of God and the Light of man."

He is the Lamb of God and the Saviour of men
which taketh away the sins of men and women
and we do need you Sweet Jesus Christ. Amen.

What a Friend and More Christ Is

VI

My life was a mess.
Life was hell I confess.
My wretched life was worthless.

I did not care then
and I was aware when
the Saviour Christ took me in.

Christ took me in
to free me from sin,
for a slave to sin I had been.

I was lost in sin,
then he found me when
my sins they numbered in tens.

I had lost my mind,
when I did then find
that he was to me kind.

Then I did find
that I was then blind,
and he made me able to see.

Jesus did set me free
and now I can see
the way to be.

Now I can see
the right way to be
thanks to Jesus you see.

He did set me free
and taught me how to be.
To be just like he is you see.

He does help me.
He does take care of me.
He does watch over and after me.

He set me free.
He rescued me
from my misery.

I did lament.
He ended my torment
and gave me purpose and intent.

God and Christ saved my soul
and then Christ made me whole.
And on them I am truthfully sold.

He is a Friend and More he is.
What a Friend and More Christ is.
And at the right hand of God Jesus is.

He is the life who commands,
with the nail-scarred-hands,
who did die for man.

He is the life and the salvation of men,
who made a stand for God's love to men and women
and we do love you Sweet Lord and Master Jesus Christ.

Amen.

What a Friend and More Christ Is

VII

My life was a mess.
Life was hell I confess.
And throughout my life, I needed some help.

I needed help when
I was sick from my sin.
And I called out to Christ Jesus for help.

I was lost in sin
I did not care then.
And he was near and did hear and did help.

Christ found me when
my sins numbered in tens.
And I was oh so glad that I had some help.

Christ took me in
to free me from sin.
And he was aware that I was there for help.

Christ took me in
to make me care again.
And I was aware that he was there for help.

Christ took me in
to give me life again.
And we were aware that I was there for help.

Christ took away my strife
to give me a more abundant life.
And throughout my life, he did certainly help.

God and Christ saved my soul
and then Christ made me whole.
And on them I am certainly sold.

He is a Friend and More he is.
What a Friend and More Christ is.
And at the right hand of God Jesus is.

"He is the true way to a more abundant life."
"He is the way, the truth, and the life."
"He is the life and he is our life."

He is our life and the Savior of men,
who paid for the sins of men and women,
and we do need you Sweet Lord Jesus. Amen.

What a Friend and More Christ Is

VIII

My life was a mess.
Life was hell I confess.
And throughout my life, I needed help.

I was lost in sin
I did not care then.
And I did call out to Christ for help.

Then he found me when
my sins did number in tens.
And without any doubt Christ did help.

He did care for me when
my life was a mess then.
And throughout my life Christ did help.

He did care for me when
I was a slave of sin then.
And then he did make me free and help.

He did care for me when
I did have no hope then.
And then he did give me hope and help.

He did care for me when
I did not even care then.
And then he did help save me and help.

God and Christ saved my soul
and then Christ made me whole.
And on them I am absolutely sold.

He is a Friend and More he is.
What a Friend and More Christ is.
And at the right hand of God Jesus is.

He gave his life for lost sinners you see,
so we might belong to his Holy Family,
and that does include you and me.

He gave his life for you and for me,
so we might have a better life you see,
and this does include a better way to be.

He gave his life as a ransom for men,
so we might have good will from God to men,
and this does include our Lord Jesus Christ. Amen.

What a Friend and More Christ Is

IX

My life was a mess.
Life was hell I confess.
And throughout my life I did need help.

I was lost in sin.
I did not care then.
And indeed he did heed my need for help.

Then he found me when
my sins did number in tens.
And he was there from nowhere to help.

I was not well then.
I was sick from sin.
And I was so glad that I had some help.

I was not aware when
I was in slavery to sin.
And he took me in and did begin to help.

Yes, he took me in
to free me from sin.
And he did help save my soul and did help.

God and Christ saved my soul
and then Christ made me whole.
And on them I am positively sold.

He is a Friend and more he is.
What a Friend and More Christ is.
And at the right hand of God Jesus is.

"He is the resurrection and the life."
"Jesus is the way, the truth, and the life."
"He came so we might have more abundant life."

He gave up his life so we might have eternal life.
And Jesus was the perfect example of life.
Jesus is the life and he is our life.

He gave up his life for the sins of men.
He lives his life for the lives of men and women.
And we do thank you Sweet Jesus for giving us life again.

He gave up his life as a ransom for men.
He did make the sacrifice for men and women.
And we do need you, Sweet Lord Jesus Christ. Amen.

*W*hat a Friend and More Christ Is

X

My life was a mess.
Life was hell I confess.
And throughout my life, I needed help.

I was lost in sin.
I did not care then.
And he did respond when I needed help.

He was aware when I needed him.
He was there when I needed him.
And he cared when I needed him.

God and Christ saved my soul
and then Christ made me whole.
And on them I am honestly sold.

He is a Friend and More he is.
What a Friend and more Christ is.
And at the right hand of God Jesus is.

He is the Son of God Elohim.
He is right there beside him.
And he always obeys him.

He is the Savior you see.
He is right of God Almighty.
And he is the only way to be.

He is the only way to be you see,
out of the two ways to be,
for you and for me.

For you and me he did die.
He gave his all and did try.
And to save us all is why.

He is worthy to be praised.
From the dead, he was raised.
There will be no end to his days.

He will defeat the beast.
He will be King of the feast.
"His kingdom will never cease."

He will live for us.
He will live for you.
He will live forever.

He died for us,
and never cussed,
our Friend Lord Jesus.

He died for us
and lives for us.
Thank you, Jesus.

What a Friend and More Christ Is

XI

My life was a mess.
Life was hell I confess.
And my wretched soul was lost.

I was lost in sin.
I did not care then.
And Christ did make up the cost.

Christ found me when
my sins did number in tens.
And I took my sins to the cross.

Christ took me in,
then forgave me my sins.
And now Jesus Christ is my Boss.

God and Christ saved my soul
and then Christ made me whole.
And on the two, I am really sold.

He is a Friend and more he is.
What a Friend and more Christ is.
And at the right hand of God Jesus is.

He is the King of the hill.
He did always God's will.
And he paid all of our bill.

He is really brave.
He did die for to save.
And he did rise from the grave.

He is really swell.
He did treat me well.
And Jesus is my Hero I do tell.

He is Shining Light.
He did treat me right.
And Jesus is my Shining Knight.

He did not entice.
He did treat me nice.
And Jesus is like sugar and spice.

He did take me in.
He saved me from sin.
And he gave me life anew again.

He had mercy on me.
He was very kind to me.
And he gave his life for me.

He gave his life for us.
He gave it his all for us.
And we love you Jesus.

He died for us.
He does live for us.
And we thank you, Jesus.

What a Friend and More Christ Is

XII

My life was a mess.
Life was hell I confess
and I was not at all blessed.

A slave I was then,
when I was lost in sin.
I could not help myself when

I wallowed in sin.
I did not care then
and I needed help when

Christ stepped in
to free me from sin
and give me life again.

God and Christ saved my soul,
and then Christ made me whole,
and on the two I am utterly sold.

He is a Friend and More he is.
What a Friend and More Christ is
And at the right hand of God Jesus is.

He is my life.
He is our life.
He is your life.

"He is the life and he is your life."
"He is the resurrection and the life."
"He is the way to a more abundant life."

"He is the way, the truth and the life you see."
"He is the way to God and the way to be you see."
"He is the only One Son of God in the trinity you see."

He is life you see.
He is life for you and me.
He is life and the way for us to be.

He gave his life and was put to death.
He laid down his life at his very last breath
and he now holds the keys to hell and death.

He is the life and the Saviour of men,
who paid the price for the sin of men
and we do need you, Jesus. Amen.

What a Friend and More Christ Is

XIII

My life was a mess.
Life was hell I confess
and I needed to be blessed.

I was lost in sin.
I did not care then
and I needed Christ when

I was sick from sin
and I had no hope then
and I needed to be born again.

Then Christ Jesus he took me in
to set my soul free from my sin
and give me life anew again.

He did set free my soul
and then he made me whole
and on Christ I am wholly sold.

He is a Friend and More he is.
What a Friend and More Christ is
And at the right hand of God Jesus is.

He is More than a Friend you see.
Christ he told us how to be.
It is up to you and me.

He is second in the trinity.
Jesus died for you and me,
so we might live for eternity.

He is eternal life.
Christ died to give us life,
and we do thank you for giving us life.

He is the life and the Saviour of men.
Christ died instead of men and women
and we do need you, Sweet Jesus. Amen.

What a Friend and More Christ Is

XIV

My life was a mess.
Life was hell I confess.
And I was tired of not being blessed.

I was tired of sin.
I did not care then.
And I looked to Christ who took me in.

He took me in
to free me from sin,
for a sinner I had been.

He did set free my soul
and Christ made me whole.
And on Christ I am entirely sold.

He is a Friend and More he is.
What a Friend and More Christ is.
And at the right hand of God Jesus is.

He is the One to look to,
no matter what you go through.
He can lighten your dark days and blues.

He is the One to go to,
when you are sad and blue.
He will always be there for you.

He is the One for you.
He will do for you.
He is for you.

He is the One who died for you
He lives his life for you.
He is life for you.

He is the One who paid dearly for your sins,
who died the death for men and women
and we do need you, Jesus. Amen.

*W*hat a Friend and More Christ Is

XV

My life was a mess.
Life was hell I confess.
And I turned to Christ to bless my soul.

I was lost in sin.
I did not care then.
And then Christ had mercy on my soul.

He did help to save my soul,
and then Christ did make me whole.
And he is merciful as we have all been told.

He is a Friend and More he is.
What a Friend and More Christ is.
And at the right hand of God Jesus is.

"He is the One and only Son of God."
"Christ is the Word of God."
"He is One with God."

"He is our intercessor and mediator with God."
"He is our creator, counselor, advocator, and advisor."
"He is our proprietor, propitiator, superior, and our Saviour."

"He is the One who we do need,"
"He is the Saviour of the world indeed."
"He is the One of who we should take heed."

He is One of two, to who we do
owe our salvation from sin to,
and life more abundantly, too.

He is the One to who we owe our life to.
He is the One to who we are devoted to.
He is the One to who we do belong to.

He is the One we go to when we are bad.
He is the One we go to when we are sad.
He is the One we go to, to make us glad.

"He is the Son of man and joy of God."
"He is the Lord of the Sabbath of God."
"He is One of the Seven Spirits of God."

"He is One of Seven."
"He is just Heaven."
"He is life's leaven."

"He is the bread of life."
"He is the water of life."
"He is the spice of life."

He is the life and the Saviour of men,
who did die in lieu of me and of you
and we do love you, Jesus. Amen.

What a Friend and More Christ Is

XVI

My life was a mess.
Life was hell I confess.
And I did need the Sinless Saviour for help.

I was lost in sin
when he found me then.
And indeed, he did heed my need for help.

He takes care of my every need
without my having to plead.
He is a Special Creed.

He did help me when
my soul was sick from sin.
He is a Friend through thick and thin.

He did help me when
my shoulders were pinned.
He is a Friend who never ever sinned.

He did help me when
my life was near an end.
He is a Friend who gave me life again.

He did help me when
my sins had done me in.
He is a Friend who is our Dear Friend.

He is a Friend and More he is.
What a Friend and More Christ is.
And at the right of the power of God is

the One you are in need of,
the One you are in reach of,
the One you are in search of,

the Lamb of God with nail-scarred hands,
who carried out God's salvation plan,
to save lost souls of men. Amen.

What a Friend and More Christ Is

XVII

My life was a mess. Life was hell I confess.
I was worthless. I was no good at all and less.
So I looked for the Sinless Saviour for help.

I was lost in sin and I was sick from sin.
Many were my sins and they numbered in tens.
Yet Christ found me and healed me and helped me in.

He took me in, my friend,
and then did begin, my friend,
to set me free from sin, my friend.

He is the good shepherd, my friend.
He was good for me, my friend
and good to me, my friend.

He is a Friend and More he is.
What a Friend and More Christ is.
And at the right hand of God Jesus is

"the only begotten Son of God,"
"the only way for us to go to God,"
"the only beloved Son, in whom God

was well pleased."
He healed the diseased
and at death, he was teased.

He won the war.
It was us he bled for.
It was our stripes he bore.

"By his stripes we are healed."
He was doing his Father's will
and he did suffer a great deal.

Yes, it was us he died for,
the sin sick, oppressed, and poor.
The One who opened salvation's door.

God's kingdom covers many lands.
His love is for more abundant than sand
and Christ is his Lamb with nail-scarred hands,

who gave his life for your salvation from sin,
who paid the price for the salvation of men,
and we love you, Great Jesus Christ. Amen.

What a Friend and More Christ Is

XVIII

My life was a mess.
Life was hell I confess.
And I went to the Saviour for help.

I was lost in sin.
I did not care then.
And Good God sent his Son to help.

I was a slave of sin.
I was a captive then.
And then he did begin

to set me free from sin
and to give me life again
and Jesus did help me then.

Although I was blind, he made me to see.
He is the One with whom I do long to be.
He was loving and caring and kind to me.

He helped me then,
when I was lost in sin,
and he is my best friend.

What a Friend and More Christ is.
He is a Friend and More he is.
And forever I will be his.

I will never forget the Cross.
I will not get over the Cross.
He was for me on the Cross.

He cried many a tear over the Cross.
Christ was heard to fear for the Cross.
He was jeered and speared on the Cross.

Jesus sweated blood over the Cross.
Christ was scourged before the Cross.
Jesus was doing God's will on the Cross.

He was on God's mission of salvation,
throughout his own nation,
without vacation.

He was the Lamb of God with nail-scarred hands,
who lived and walked on earth in flesh as man,
and preached the kingdom of God to man.

It was a glorious time when he walked on earth,
some thirty-two years after his very special birth.
And he did fill my heart and my soul with mirth.

He is my life and the Saviour of men,
who did die in place of men and women
and then Jesus Christ did rise again. Amen.

*W*hat a Friend and More Christ Is

XIX

I was sick from sin.
For a sinner I had been.
And one sinner can destroy much good.

I was on my last leg.
For my existence I did beg.
And I was very bad and up to no good.

I was stressed out.
I could not chill out.
And I did not have a very good life.

I tried to end my life.
I could not handle the strife.
And I did honestly need a good wife.

My life was a bore.
I had nothing to live for.
And I could not stand it anymore.

My life was a harrow.
I had nothing but sorrow.
And I thought there was no tomorrow.

My life was a shamble.
Life for me was a gamble.
To change my life, I was just unable.

My life was a mess.
Life for me was stress.
Yes, for me, life seemed hopeless.

I was lost in sin.
I did not care then.
Yet Christ cared when

I had no hope
and I could not cope.
I was at the end of my rope

but Christ is a Friend and More he is.
What a Friend and More Christ is
and he is for you and me he is.

He is tender, loving, and kind to me.
He taught me to be like he is you see,
and he made me to see the way to be.

"He is the way, the truth, and the life,
who did live by God's law all his life,
and Jesus is the Light of my life."

He is the life who is our very Kind Friend,
who did give his life for your and our sins,
and we do love you, Master Jesus. Amen.

What a Friend and More Christ Is

XX

I was lost in sin.
I was sick from sin.
And I sincerely tell you, I was not well and I needed some
    help then.

My life was a mess.
Life was hell I confess.
And I tell you, Christ treated me well and healed me and
    helped me.

He did operate on me without a knife,
and took away my troubles and strife,
and he gave me hope and a new life.

He gave me a new life,
and the hope of a good wife,
and he made me sharp as a knife.

He put my feet on solid ground.
He made my mind and body sound.
He did all this and turned my life around.

"He did give his life so we all might have eternal life."
"He came so we might have more abundant life."
"He is the way, and the truth and the life."

"He is the Saviour, the Messiah, the bread of life."
"He is the Healer, the Messiah, the water of life."
"He is the One, the Only, and the spice of life."

He is a Friend and More he is.
What a Friend and More Christ is.
And at the right of the power of God is

"the life and the Son of God,"
"the life and the Word of God,"
"the life and the Lamb of God,"

the life and the Hope of men and women,
who gave his life for the sins of men
and we love you, Jesus. Amen.

What a Friend and More Christ Is

XXI

I was lost in sin.
I did not care then.
I was not aware when

I was guilty as sin.
I was all done in.
I could not win.

I was out on a limb.
I could not get to God Elohim
because you see no man gets to God except by him.

I had made a mess.
I needed help I confess.
So I accepted the Saviour for forgiveness and help.

My life was a mess.
Life was hell I confess.
Yet he forgave me my sins and did begin to help.

He has power on earth to forgive sins
and he did forgive my sins,
when he took me in.

Though my sins were many,
even though my sins were plenty,
and although my sins were in twenties,

he took me in, my friend,
and then did begin, my friend,
to set me free from sin, my friend.

Yes Christ was there, my friend,
and he was aware, my friend,
and he did care, my friend.

In my heart and mind, he was kind you see,
and although I was blind, he made me to see,
and I would like to be exactly like Jesus you see,

because he is the way to be,
the way, the truth, and the life you see,
and the only way to God for forgiveness for you and for me.

He is a Friend and More he is.
What a Friend and More Christ is.
And at the right hand of God Jesus is.

He is the Son who forgives our sins.
He is the Messiah who never sinned.
He is the Saviour "who knew no sin."

He is Hosanna and the Saviour of men,
who made the sacrifice for your and our sins,
and we love you, Saviour of men and women. Amen.

What a Friend and More Christ Is

XXII

My life was a mess.
Life was hell I confess.
And I needed a beating I guess.

I was lost in sin.
I did not care then,
when I was a slave of sin.

I was sin sick.
I was getting my kicks.
Yet he did choose and pick me

to serve.
I did not deserve.
Yet he did throw me a curve

and gave me a commission
by a messenger as I listened.
One would think that I glistened.

I said, "He might choose me
but I don't choose him."
Yet he chose me.

This is the way he is,
the way he is
always.

And the way, the truth, and the light,
at the right of the power of God's might,
he helped to save me that special night.

He helped save my life
at the point of a knife.
He took away strife.

He helped saved my soul
and then he made me whole.
And on Jesus Christ I am sold.

What a Friend and More he is.
What a Friend and More Christ is.
And at the right hand of God Jesus is.

"He is the One and Only Son of God."
"He is the One and Only Word of God."
"He is the One and Only Lamb of God."

He is the One who helped me in.
He is the One who helped save me from sin.
He is the One who helped to get me life anew again,

who paid the price for men and women,
who made a stand for God's love to men
and we love you, Lord Jesus Christ. Amen.

What a Friend and More Christ Is

XXIII

Satan was after me.
He had nearly got me.
So then I looked up and called out to God to help me.

Satan was no friend.
He had demised my end,
when God's only begotten Son called Christ helped me.

In my heart, he did put a song.
He made me feel as though I belonged
and Jesus made me able to tell right from wrong.

He is a Friend and More he is.
What a Friend and More Christ is.
And to the right of the power of God is

the One with the two nail-scarred hands
who died in lieu of the sins of man
and we are yours and so is man,

the One who is more precious than pearls
who died for the sins of the world
and we are his boys and girls,

the One who is our guide
who died and never lied
and he is on your side,

the One for me and you,
who does for us, too
and we do love you.

the One who is our very Dear Friend,
who paid the price for your and our sins
and we do love you, Lord Jesus Christ. Amen.

What a Friend and More Christ Is

XXIV

My life was a mess.
Life was hell I confess.
So I looked up to God for help.

I was lost in sin.
I did not care then,
when God's Son Jesus did help.

I was sick from sin,
when Christ took me in
and then made me healthy again.

He made my mind and body sound.
He made my mountains seem like mounds.
He did all this for me and he turned my life around.

He is a Friend and More he is.
What a Friend and More Christ is.
And at the right of the power of God is

the One who shines very bright,
the way, the truth, and the light,
the anointed One who is always right.

the one who is worthy of fame,
who knows all our names,
and has no blame,

the One who took me by the hand,
who against Satan made a stand,
and I think he is really grand,

the One who took me in, my friend,
who set me free from sin, my friend
and gave to me life again, my friend,

the One who is our very Dear Friend,
who paid the price for the world's sin
and we do love you, Lord Jesus. Amen.

*W*hat a Friend and More Christ Is

XXV

My life was a mess.
Life was hell I confess.
I had absolutely no happiness.
I could not handle all the stress.
And I was completely full of loneliness.

I thought of Myself.
I thought of no one else.
And I had no health or wealth.
I could not help my helplessness.
Then I called out to Jehovah for help.

I was lost in sin.
I did not care then.
I was not aware when
I was in slavery to sin then,
when Jesus Christ took me in.

And for a start
he made me smart.
He worked on my heart
and Jesus did it with an art,
up until our ways they did part.

He very nearly blew my mind.
He broke the shackles that did bind.
He made me to see, although I was blind.
I was hopelessly lost when me Jesus did find.
And to my heart and mind Jesus was oh so kind.

He was more kind than a holy kiss.
No one was ever more kind than this
and he filled my heart with more bliss.
Until he returns, we will evermore miss.
What a Friend and More Jesus Christ is.

Christ is considerate and compassionate.
he is our rock, refuge, and righteousness.
He is mighty, marvelous, and miraculous.
He is worthy, wondrous, and wonderful.
What a Friend and More Jesus Christ is.

"Christ is the way and the truth and the Prince of life."
"He is the Saviour, the Messiah, the bread of life."
"He is the healer, the helper, the water of life."
"He is the One, the Only, the spice of life."
What a Friend and More Jesus Christ is.

Christ is the bright and morning star.
He is light but he died for the dark.
He is all right and he cares how you are.
He is always right and never harps.
And right of God Almighty from afar is

Jesus who made a stand,
who is both Great and Grand.
He carried out God's salvation plan
to save the lost souls of woman and man.
He is the Lamb of God with pierced side and hands.
Amen

What a Friend and More Christ Is

XXVI

Halo
My name is Wes.
This is my address.
My life was a total mess.
I had absolutely no happiness.
My life was that of utter sadness.
I was full of loneliness and emptiness.
My aimless purpose in life was meaningless
and I played around like life was one big recess.

From my early childhood, I did regress.
Trouble was one continual process.
I did make trouble my business.
I made practically no progress.
I was no good at all and less.
I was certainly no success.
I was under great stress.
I was deep depressed.
I was hard-pressed.

I was in dire distress.
I had no physical fitness.
I had positively no finesse.
I was sorry and God is my witness.
I was like an animal in the wilderness.
My disturbed feelings I could not express.
To cigarettes, alcohol, and drugs I had access.
My drug and alcohol habit, I could not repress.
I carried everything to the extreme and excess.

I did live, think, and drive reckless.
I was careless, hopeless, and Godless.
I was determined to have my way regardless.
I was fruitless and shiftless and worthless.
I was not at all blameless, but I was shameless.
I was heartless, I was mindless, and I was pitiless.
I was pitiful, fearful, frightful, and spiteful.
I was ungrateful and unfaithful and unmerciful.
I was deceitful, disrespectful, hateful, and vengeful.

I was sexually aggressive.
My sex drive was incessant.
I always wanted the unnecessary.
Sex and not love I made a necessity
and my lustful urge I could not suppress
and I went after most all females in a dress.
Most all girls and women I did try to impress
and with a female prostitute I did try to caress.
The only thing not in my life was a kept mistress.

From a married woman I caught the ick
My outlook and attitude was pessimistic.
My perspective on life was not optimistic.
I was demonic, sadistic, and I was satanic.
I was a physical wreck, neurotic, and psychotic.
I was allergic and apathetic and I was pathetic.
I was erotic and erratic and I was not energetic.
I was not at all apologetic, sympathetic, or patriotic.
I could not even rhyme nor was I poetically inclined.

I was in a mental recession.
I had a very sad expression.
I left an extremely bad impression.
I made sin in my life an obsession.
I was financially in a deep depression
and with my friends I was suppressive.
My appearance was not very impressive.
Some parts of my hairline were recessive
and two of my teeth were dark from abscess.

I walked in darkness.
I was not at all blessed.
I was suddenly possessed.
With Satan, I did have a session
and I did become Satan's successor.
I needed Jesus Christ the intercessor.
Against Jehovah my maker I did transgress
and against almost everyone else I did trespass
and very nearly everyone was angry with me I guess.

My life was hell I confess.
I could not handle the stress.
No, I could not help my helplessness.
So I called out to God Almighty for help.

I was a slave of sin.
I did not behave then.
And I did not care when
a troublemaker I had been.

I was lost in sin.
I did not care then.
I was in slavery to sin,
when his Son took me in.

Yes, Yahweh did send his Best,
his Word manifested in flesh,
his Son full of virtue and zest,
so we might have eternal rest.

Yes, Jesus his Son from his heart, he did send,
his only begotten Son who would not bend,
even though with sinners he did blend,
so as to start us on a new trend.

For his Father and for us he came,
to endure the suffering and the pain.
He and his Father were one in the same,
Alleluia, with no blame, praise their names.

He resisted every temptation
with persistence and determination.
Then he went through Father-Son separation
and for this reason, the Lord Jesus Christ is a sensation.

He was all alone.
He was on his own.
He was all by himself.
He was something else.

He was always correct and perfect
and his Father Abba, Jesus did reflect.
And some people, they showed him respect,
while other people, Jesus Christ they did reject.

He was born in Bethlehem
and he turned the world upside down.
And then he was crucified outside of Jerusalem,
after the Lord Jesus Christ turned sinners' lives around.

With Satan he did compete,
until his work was complete,
until nailed both hands and feet.
A feat no one could ever repeat.

He fed us more than bread.
"Live right," the Rabbi said,
one of the triune Godhead
who was raised from the dead.

He did pull the grade.
Now he does have it made.
He made it to the top.
Now he cares for us a lot.

He does live for us now.
He loves us and how.
He does live for you,
no one else will do.

He never ever sleeps.
He tends to his sheep.
He tends to us,
our Friend Jesus.

He is a Friend and More he is.
What a Friend and More he is.
And forevermore we will be his.
And seated right of our God he is.

He is our inspiration.
He is our perspiration.
He is our circulation.
He is our respiration.

He is our superior and counselor.
He is our instructor and interceptor.
He is our propitiator and intercessor.
He is our intermediator and mediator.

He is master and leader.
He is preacher and teacher.
He is minister and manager.
He is commander and server.

He is servant and savant.
He is radiant and valiant.
He is gallant and elegant.
He is chalant and tolerant.

He is pleasant and observant.
He is important and consultant.
He is concordant and brilliant.
He is significant and exuberant.

He is excited and experienced.
He is excelled and expertized.
He is extolled and exemplified.
He is exalted and exonerated.

He is immaculate and compassionate.
He is considerate and affectionate.
He is articulate and appropriate.
He is first-rate and first mate.

He is the top.
He is top Son.
He is topmost.
He is top flight.

He is top kick.
He is top brass.
He is top level.
He is top dollar.

He is well-favored.
He is well-advised.
He is well-informed.
He is well-appointed.

He is well-beloved.
He is well-behaved.
He is well-balanced.
He is well-rounded.

He is smooth-tongued.
He is straight-ahead.
He is sober-minded.
He is single-minded.

He is single-hearted and openhearted.
He is tenderhearted and truehearted.
He is warm-blooded and long-lived.
He is foresighted and open-eyed.

He was crucified and he died.
He was resurrected and lives.
He is dignified and concerned.
He is sanctified and consecrated.

He is sacred and adored.
He is devoted and assured.
He is learned and educated.
He is blessed and behooved.

He is needed and heeded.
He is cherished and venerated.
He is dedicated and determined.
He is accomplished and distinguished.

He is bequeathed and believed.
He is civilized and cultured.
He is mannered and spirited.
He is hallowed and glorified.

He is glorious and generous.
He is fabulous and famous.
He is humorous and precious.
He is cautious and serious.

He is virtuous and sedulous.
He is courteous and ingenious.
He is righteous and courageous.
He is stupendous and tremendous.

He is miraculous and marvelous.
He is mellifluous and magnanimous.
He is pretentious and superfluous.
He is conspicuous and conscientious.

He is illustrious and efficacious.
He is spontaneous and harmonious.
He is factitious and gracious.
He is victorious and wondrous.

He is wonderful and useful.
He is regardful and restful.
He is masterful and rightful.
He is bountiful and plentiful.

He is artful and lawful.
He is helpful and careful.
He is fearful and tearful.
He is hopeful and mindful.

He is tactful and tuneful.
He is willful and wishful.
He is wakeful and watchful.
He is cheerful and skillful.

He is peaceful and powerful.
He is graceful and merciful.
He is tasteful and grateful.
He is faithful and fruitful.

He is thankful and trustful.
He is truthful and thoughtful.
He is delightful and meaningful.
He is respectful and resourceful.

He is "King of kings."
He is loving and caring.
He is giving and sharing.
He is moving and amusing.

He is amazing and exciting.
He is becoming and charming.
He is pleasing and spanking.
He is appealing and consoling.

He is forgiving and promising.
He is motivating and gratifying.
He is deserving and rewarding.
He is captivating and fascinating.

He is astounding and encouraging.
He is convincing and law-abiding.
He is refreshing and enchanting.
He is intriguing and compelling.

He is interesting and accommodating.
He is outstanding and understanding.
He is enlightening and illuminating.
He is earthshaking and electrifying.

He is electric and fantastic.
He is majestic and magnetic.
He is prophetic and empathetic.
He is scientific and sympathetic.

He is specific and analytic.
He is authentic and terrific.
He is heroic and hypnotic.
He is poetic and dynamic.

He is poetry and holy.
He is tidy and ready.
He is canny and funny.
He is handy and happy.

He is spry and merry.
He is lusty and mighty.
He is catchy and folksy.
He is classy and sanity.

He is sanitary and authority.
He is legendary and extraordinary.
He is noteworthy and trustworthy.
He is thankworthy and praiseworthy.

He is worthy and lively.
He is steady and sturdy.
He is speedy and sporty.
He is hearty and kindly.

He is nifty and spiffy.
He is sparky and swifty.
He is jiffy and biffy.
He is ziffy and zippy.

He is healthy and wealthy.
He is thrifty and orderly.
He is liberty and quality.
He is heavenly and royalty.

He is royal and loyal.
He is moral and total.
He is normal and social.
He is actual and factual.

He is capital and cordial.
He is musical and special.
He is natural and neutral.
He is logical and magical.

He is eternal and immortal.
He is original and unusual.
He is punctual and personal.
He is rational and practical.

He is emotional and essential.
He is triumphal and spiritual.
He is effectual and economical.
He is perpetual and proverbial.

He is professional and intellectual.
He is fundamental and instrumental.
He is satisfactual and circumstantial.
He is consequential and transcendental.

He is phenomenal and beneficial.
He is substantial and influential.
He is sensational and exceptional.
He is theological and reverential.

He is reverent and patient.
He is affluent and prudent.
He is obedient and diligent.
He is efficient and excellent.

He is confident and competent.
He is beneficent and benevolent.
He is sufficient and independent.
He is intelligent and magnificent.

He is attentive and active.
He is assertive and motive.
He is effective and objective.
He is executive and exclusive.

He is appreciative and constructive.
He is contemplative and instructive.
He is constitutive and productive.
He is imaginative and affirmative.

He is creative and positive.
He is positive and inventive.
He is decisive and conclusive.
He is impressive and sensitive.

He is sensible and credible and incredible.
He is invincible and accessible and compatible.
He is incorruptible and indivisible and perceptible.
He is comprehensible and irresistible and responsible.

He is able and capable.
He is stable and affable.
He is durable and amiable.
He is loveable and notable.

He is valuable and laudable.
He is suitable and sociable.
He is peaceable and honorable.
He is memorable and reliable.

He is tolerable and agreeable.
He is charitable and admirable.
He is impeccable and dependable.
He is presentable and respectable.

He is conceivable and commendable.
He is incomparable and considerable.
He is approachable and knowledgeable.
He is impressionable and distinguishable.

He is seasonable and reasonable.
He is hospitable and noticeable.
He is remarkable and believable.
He gives to his joy unspeakable.

For us he has very many plans.
The Ruler of the very many lands.
The Lamb with the nail-scarred hands.
And his love is for more bountiful than sand.

The Most High Priest with many crowns,
who knows no red, white, yellow, black, or brown,
and the Lord he will never put you down,
and he will never put on your face a fret or frown.

The exception of men.
The salvation of men.
The redemption of men.
We do love you. Amen.

What a Friend and More Christ Is

XXVII

My life was a mess.
Life was hell I confess.
I was empty of loneliness
and I was full of emptiness.

I just thought
I was tough stuff.
I was naught.
I was a cream puff.

I used to be mean.
I was a bad dream.
I was in midstream.
I was a loud scream.

I was a sight.
I lived by night.
I did not do right.
I had very little light.

I had no hope.
I could not cope.
I was addicted to dope.
I was at the end of my rope.

I thought, *What was the use?*
I lived my life very reclusive.
I was myself physically abusive.
To end my life, I was conclusive.

I have often asked to die
and here is the reason why.
I have lived a life of hell
and I was not at all well.

I had failed nearly every test.
I had not even tried my best.
I did make of myself a pest,
so I looked up to the Best.

And his Immortal and Immaculate Son Emmanuel
took me in to set me free from sin and on my
immorality and immaturity he immediately
did begin to go to work on from within.

Yes, suddenly he was there my friend
from out of nowhere, my friend
and I was aware, my friend
that he cared, my friend.

He put my feet on solid ground.
He made my mind and body sound.
He made me sane and I put on pounds.
He made my mountains seem like mounds.
He did all this for me and turned my life around
and in my heart and my mind, he is truly astounding.

What a Friend and More Christ is.
And at the right of the power of God is
the Friend who helped save me from sin,
and he has never let us down or done us in,
the One who gave his life as ransom for men,
and we do love you Saviour Jesus Christ. Amen.

𝒲hat a Friend and More Christ Is

XXVIII

My life was a mess.
Life was hell I confess.
I had absolutely no happiness
and I was completely full of emptiness.

My life was hell.
I was not well.
I was sin sick
by my kicks.

"My head was in the clouds"
and "I was not down-to-earth."
"I was running again the wind"
and "I was headed for hellfire."

I was a liar
and feared not the fire.
I was a cheat
and feared not the heat.

I was beat
and not neat.
I was weak
and not meek.

I was flesh
and not spirit.
I was fresh
and not with it.

I was dumb
and not bright.
I was dark
and not light.

I was silly
and not serious.
I was giddy
and not cautious.

I was unrighteous
and not righteous.
I was unfaithful
and not faithful.

I was incomplete
and not discreet.
I was disgraceful
and not graceful.

I was hell
and not well.
I was reeling
and not healing.

I was falling
and not feeling.
I was appalling
and not appealing.

I was negative
and not positive.
I was destructive
and not constructive.

I was lonely
and not alone.
I was lonesome
and not twosome.

I was conceited
and not needed.
I was conquered
and not heeded.

I was pessimistic
and not optimistic.
I was totalistic
and not futuristic.

I was outback
and not upfront.
I was down and out
and not up and at 'em.

I was backward
and not forward.
I was a coward
and not onward.

I was a fool
and not cool.
I was a scamp
and not champ.

I was a rogue
and not vogue.
I was a peasant
and not pleasant.

I was a heathen
with no rhyme or reason.
I was full of strife
with no purpose to my life.

I was a wretch.
I was a letch.
I was a witch.
I was a snitch.

I was not nice.
I had head lice.
I was prejudiced.
I had many a vice.

I was not tenderhearted
and I was hard-hearted.
I was not warm-hearted
and I was cold-hearted.

I was not glad
and I was sad.
I was not true
and I was blue.

"I was green with envy."
"I was not tickled pink."
"I was not in the black"
and "I was not rosy red."

"I was fruity."
"I was bananas."
"I was a lemon."
"I was not the apple of his eye."

"I was sour."
"I was bitter."
"I was not sweet."
"I was not the salt of the earth."

"I was a goldbricker."
"I was as cold as ice."
"I had a heart of stone."
"I did not have all my marbles."

"I was lonely."
"I was a phony."
"I thought of me only."
"I did find myself full of baloney."

I was terrible.
I was horrible.
I was miserable.
To save myself, I was really unable.

I was weary.
I did not try.
I was teary.
I did not cry.

I was cheap.
I did not give.
I was bleak.
I did not live.

I did take.
I was a fake.
I was a snake.
I was all hate.

I did steal.
I was not real.
I had no appeal.
I sinned a great deal.

I was lost in sin.
I did not care then.
I was in slavery to sin,
when his Son took me in.

He came to my rescue
and he was right on cue.
He turned my gray skies to blue.
He was very kind and this is true.

He gave me life anew again.
He helped save me from sin,
although I was not aware when
he did all this for me back then.

He cleansed my soul and my heart.
He gave my life a brand-new start.
He decorated me like a work of art
and all that I had to do was my part.

He had my name called from way up high in a tree.
Now I know you may find this hard to believe
but he honestly called my name through the leaves
and now I know that he really did care for me.

He loved me through songs,
even when I had done wrong.
He made me feel that I belonged
and now for him, I do honestly long.

What a Friend and More Jesus the Christ is.
No one has ever been more of a Friend than this.
I do honestly look forward to the day when I am his.
And directly to the right of the Greatest of all Jesus is

"the way and the truth and the life,"
"the One, the Only, and the spice of life,"
"the Saviour, the Messiah, the water of life,"
"the Healer, the Helper, and the bread of life,"

the Friend who helped save me from sin,
who gave his life as a ransom for men,
who paid the price for the world's sin
and we do love you, Jesus. Amen.

What a Friend and More Christ Is

XXIX

My life was a mess.
Life was hell I confess.
I really had no happiness.
I was no good at all and less.

I was worthless.
I was shiftless.
I was reckless.
I was shameless.

I was joyless.
I was jobless.
I was fruitless.
I was homeless.

I was hopeless.
I was helpless.
I was hairless.
I was hapless.

I was heartless.
I was brainless.
I was careless.
I was pitiless.

I was pitiful.
I was harmful.
I was needful.
I was wasteful.

I was awful.
I was hateful.
I was spiteful.
I was deceitful.

I was lying.
I was dying.
I was crying.
I was sighing.

I was dependent.
I was belligerent.
I was negligent.
I was deficient.

I was defiant.
I was stagnant.
I was flippant.
I was nonchalant.

I was vulgar.
I was a voyeur.
I was voluptuous.
I was vulnerable.

I was venomous.
I was vengeful.
I was vindictive.
I was vindicated.

I was perverted.
I was subverted.
I was diverted.
I was converted.

I was ill-behaved.
I was ill-natured.
I was ill-mannered.
I was ill-tempered.

I was self-centered.
I was self-conscious.
I was self-righteous.
I was self-destructive.

I was selfish.
I was impish.
I was broodish.
I was devilish.

I was possessed.
I was obsessed.
I was repressed.
I was depressed.

I was suicidal.
I was homicidal.
I was radical.
I was habitual.

I was psychologically in.
I was intellectually out.
I was mentally down.
I was logically off.

I was socially bad.
I was physically had.
I was emotionally mad.
I was individually a cad.

I was morally corrupt.
I was personally abrupt.
I was spiritually bankrupt.
I would, at anything, erupt.

I was an ass.
I was asinine.
I was a behind.
I would not mind.

I was irate.
I was obstinate.
I was degenerate.
I could not concentrate.

I was furious and curious.
I was anxious and obnoxious.
I was dubious and oblivious.
I was monstrous and ridiculous.

I was erotic and irregular.
I was erratic and irrational.
I was irrelevant and irreverent.
I was irreligious and irresponsible.

I was impure and impious.
I was immoral and immature.
I was immodest and improper.
I was impudent and imprudent.

I was impatient and imperfect.
I was impractical and impossible.
I was impetuous and imbalanced.
I was impertinent and impersonal.

I was inapt and inept.
I was insane and intense.
I was inexact and insipid.
I was inferior and insincere.

I was indirect and incorrect.
I was inartistic and inexplicit.
I was inhumane and insecure.
I was insanitary and inexperienced.

I was incomplete and indiscrete.
I was incapacious and insidious.
I was injurious and incautious.
I was infamous and incongruous.

I was incoherent and inadvertent.
I was incompetent and indifferent.
I was insufficient and inefficient.
I was inconsistent and indecent.

I was incessant and indignant.
I was incognizant and insignificant.
I was intemperate and inadequate.
I was inconsiderate and insubordinate.

I was inappropriate and inexpressive.
I was inappreciative and indecisive.
I was inapprehensive and insensitive.
I was inapprehensible and insensible.

I was incorrigible and incomprehensible.
I was incompatible and incontrollable.
I was inexcusable and inhospitable.
I was intolerable and incapable.

I was incapable and unstable.
I was invaluable and unlovable.
I was unreasonable and ineffable.
I was undependable and unreliable.

I was unbearable and unsuitable.
I was unsociable and unfavorable.
I was undesirable and unbelievable.
I was uncomfortable and uncharitable.

I was unapt and unfit.
I was unjust and unfair.
I was untrue and unkind.
I was unclean and uncouth.

I was unaware and unsound.
I was unwise and uncertain.
I was unpopular and unwholesome.
I was unpleasant and unscrupulous.

I was unreal and unrealistic.
I was unruly and unfriendly.
I was uncanny and unsteady.
I was unhappy and unworthy.

I was ungodly and unrighteous.
I was unholy and unreligious.
I was unmoral and ungracious.
I was uncivil and ungenerous.

I was uncivilized, unadvised, and unbalanced.
I was uncommitted, unconcerned, and undecided.
I was unorganized, unreserved, and unaccomplished.
I was underhanded, undermined, and underprivileged.

I was unsettled and unnerving.
I was unfeeling and unending.
I was unavailing and uninteresting.
I was unbecoming and unforgiving.

I was unmerciful and unlawful.
I was unmindful and untruthful.
I was unfruitful and unthankful.
I was ungrateful and unfaithful.

I was distrustful, distasteful, and distressful.
I was disdainful, disrespectful, and disgraceful.
I was distraught, disobedient, and disorderly.
I was dishonest, disloyal, and discombobulated.

I was disturbed, disorganized, and discontented.
I was disinclined, disinterested, and dismayed.
I was dispelled, disappointed, and dissatisfied.
I was disabled, disagreeable, and dishonorable.

I was disgusting and discouraging.
I was disarming and disheartening.
I was discriminating and disastrous.
I was discourteous and disingenuous.

I was ambidextrous and obnoxious.
I was cantankerous and ludicrous.
I was contemptuous and ridiculous.
I was contradictious and rebellious.

I was lazy.
I was crazy.
I was sassy.
I was brassy.

I was biased.
I was bizarre.
I was berserk.
I was a jerk.

I was rude.
I was crude.
I was stewed.
I was a prude.

I was a put-on.
I was a carry-on.
I was a put-off.
I was a show-off.

I was a sexist.
I was a racist.
I was a defeatist.
I was a concede-ist.

I was a worm.
I was a germ.
I was a bum.
I was a crumb.

I was a fool.
I was a ghoul.
I was a hunky.
I was a junky.

I was a nut.
I was a rut.
I was a butt.
I had no guts.

I was a wimp.
I was a blimp.
I was a care actor.
I had no character.

I was a punk.
I was a drunk.
I was a skunk.
I had no spunk.

I loved money.
I had no honey.
I loved lust.
I had no trust.

I had no health nor no wealth.
I though of Myself and no one else.
I thought I was beyond help and helpless.
So I looked up and called out to God for help.

I was lost in sin.
I did not care then.
I was in slavery to sin.
when his Son took me in.

He took all my guilt away.
The price for my sins he did pay
and I certainly do honestly hope and pray
that the next time Jesus is with me he will stay.

I would like to be Jesus's knight.
He healed me both day and night
and he straightened out my bad life
but he did not promise me a good life.

He healed my "heart of stone"
and he made me "to feel at home"
and he made me "feel I was not alone"
and he made me "stop being accident prone."

What a Friend and More Jesus Christ is.
He mists the flowers and true is this.
He has powers and he is bliss.
He is ours and we are his.

He is swell and this we do think.
He is the well from which we drink.
He did walk on water and did not sink.
And our chain and our link to our God is

a Friend who helped save us from sin,
who gave his life as a ransom for men,
who paid the price for the world's sin
and we do love you Lord Jesus. Amen.

What a Friend and More Christ Is

XXX

My life was a mess.
Life was hell I confess.
I had absolutely no happiness.
I was completely full of emptiness
and I was in very much deep, dire distress.

"I was full of bull."
"I was full of baloney."
"I was full of me only."
"I was full of Myself"
and full of no one else.

"I was going to where fast."
"I was living life in the fast lane."
"I lived life like there was no tomorrow."
"I was burning the candle at both the ends"
and "I was up night late burning the midnight oil."

"I was barely getting by."
"I could not make ends meet."
"I could not pull my own weight."
"I could not really get it together"
and "I was coming apart at the seams."

"I was as tight as a tick."
"I was mean as a snake."
"I was drunk as a skunk."
"I was not fit as a fiddle"
and "I had an ax to grind."

"I was not hanging loose."
"I was bad, I was not good."
"I was no winner, I was a loser."
"I simply could not win for losing."
Christ, I should have been choosing.

I was forward.
I was a four-flusher
and I did the forbidden.
I did average many a fifth
and I ate entirely too much food.

"I was three sheets in the wind."
"I had three strikes against me."
"I was down for a three count."
"I was out for the count of ten."
"I was a zero on a scale of ten."

"I was a two-timer."
"I was a two-time loser."
"I was in a hurry double-time."
I was working Sunday overtime
and I was sentenced to jail one time.

I did need help.
"I could not make it."
"I was merely existing."
"I was angry at the world."
I was as worldly as could be."

"I tried to whip the world
single-handed" you see.
I was not single-minded.
I was not single-hearted.
I was single and lonesome.

"One was the loneliest number."
"I thought that I was number one."
"I thought that I was the only one."
"I was not in oneness with anyone."
"I had a one-track mind, sex or sin.

I was lost in sin.
I did not care then.
I was not aware when
I was in slavery to sin then,
when his Son Jesus took me in.

He did turn me around.
He took away my frown.
He did settle me down.
He took away my anxiety.
He did it with propriety.

He straightened out my life.
He put hope and joy in my life.
He took hate and fear out of my life.
He put health and happiness in my life.
He took sorrow and suffering out of my life.

He suffered and bled for me.
He gave his life and died for me.
He surrendered his will to God's for me.
He helped save my wretched lost soul for me,
so that I might live life and be happy for all eternity.

He is a Friend and More he is.
What a Friend and More Christ is.
And at the right hand of God Jesus is.
He is the number One Son of God he is.
And for ever and evermore we all will be his.

He is the Lamb of God and the redemption of men,
whose blood was shed for remission of the sins of men
and the Word of God, which taketh away the sins of men
and he gave his life as a ransom for the world of men and
    women
and we do need and love you, Lord and Master Jesus
    Christ. Amen.

What a Friend and More Christ Is

XXXI

My life was a mess.
Life was hell I confess.
I was empty of loneliness.
I had absolutely no happiness.
I was completely full of emptiness.

I was in trouble and Satan had busted my bubble.
"I was in a rut" and I could not shake that big nut.
"I was lower than a snake in a wagon wheel rut."
I was low-minded, low-hearted, and low-spirited.
I was lowly, and I felt low and I was low-down.

I was downcast.
I was downhearted.
I was downtrodden.
I was not down-to-earth
and I was down and out.

"I was not up to snuff."
"I was far from par and uptight."
"I was up the creek without a paddle."
"I was no good" and "I was up to no good."
"I did not know what was up or what was going down."

I was in deep water over my head.
I was overburdened and overbearing.
I was overanxious and overconfident.
I was overtaken, overrun, overcome
and I was overworked and underpaid.

I was under great stress.
I was under the bad weather.
I was underdeveloped and underfed.
I was misunderstood and the underdog
and I was underhanded and undermined.

I was not open-minded.
I was close-minded.
I was not openhanded.
I was "tightfisted."
I was not openhearted.

I messed around.
I horsed around.
I played around.
I fooled around
and I ran around.

"I was not tuned in or turned on."
"I was a put on and a carry on."
"I was not on the ball at all."
"I was not right on the nose."
"I got off on the wrong foot."

"I was off my rocker."
"I was not well-off."
"I was a little off."
"I was a lot off."
"I was off sides."

"I was off base."
"I did goof off."
"I was ticked off."
"I put things off."
"I was really off."

"I was out of bounds and way out."
"I was out by a mile and far out."
"I was out of tune and put out."
"I was out cold and strung out."
"I was out of it and spaced out."

"I was out of touch."
"I was out of control."
"I was really out of hand."
"I was totally out of my mind."
"I was outrageous and outlandish."

"I was not outstanding."
"I was outmaneuvered."
"I was outnumbered."
"I was outsmarted."
"I was outfoxed."

"I had a bad outlook on life."
"I was outranked and outcast."
"I was an out and out outsider."
"I was given to sudden outbursts."
"I was not outgoing nor was outright."

I was going the wrong way.
I was a way out outlaw.
I was way out of line.
I was out of the way.
I was way behind.

I wasted time.
I was seldom on time.
I was nearly always late.
I did not keep dates.
I was all hate.

"I was not tender."
"I was a pretender."
"I was an elbow bender."
To God, I would not surrender
and God's good work I did hinder.

"I was not cool."
"I played the fool."
"I played dirty pool."
"I broke every rule"
and sin was my tool.

I was lost in sin.
I did not care then.
I was not aware when
I was in slavery to sin then.
I did not know where to begin

to look for help.
I had not health,
I had not wealth,
and with Satan I had dealt.
So I looked up to God for help.

His Son did relieve
and put my mind at ease.
He cured me of my disease
without my having to ask please.
He cured me from my disease of sin.

He made me sane
and without any pain,
without medical training.
He put me in the right lane
and in his debt I will remain.

He made me feel fine.
He made me feel divine.
He was kinder than kind.
He healed my body and mind
and it did not take much time.

What a Friend and More Christ is.
The Christ who is our Dear Friend,
who paid the price for the world's sin
and which taketh away the sins of men
and we do love you, Jesus Christ. Amen.

What a Friend and More Christ Is

XXXII

My life was a mess.
Life was hell I confess.
I had absolutely no happiness.
I was a physical and mental mess.

"I was out of my mind and I would not mind."
"I would not mind my own business."
"I was a hair-raising experience"
and I was losing my hair.

I was scatterbrained.
I was headstrong.
I was hardheaded.
I was bullheaded.

"I had not a good head on my shoulders."
"I was in no way at the head of my class."
"I could barely keep my head above water"
And "I was drowning in my own deep sorrow."

I had a hot temper and a cold heart.
I did not "put my heart above my head."
I was a heartbreaker and I had no heart.
I was brainless and thoughtless and heartless.

I was coldhearted.
I was hard-hearted.
I was dark-hearted.
I was brokenhearted.

"I had no sense of right and wrong."
"I had all the unmitigated gall."
"I had all the nerve" and
"my nerves were shot."

"I had no appeal and I had no zeal."
"I was not real and I could not feel."
"I had no feelings and I had no taste."
"I was a pain and I had no inner beauty."

"I had no guts,"
and "no fortitude"
and "I had a weak stomach,"
and "I could not stomach much."

"I was stiff-necked."
"I was a backstabber."
"I had a monkey on my back."
"I had no backbone and I was spineless."

"I was cold-shouldered."
"I had a chip on my shoulder."
"I had the world on my shoulders"
and "I had no strong shoulder to cry on."

I had tried not to cry.
I had tried not to sigh.
I had tried not to lie.
I had tried, my oh my.

"I could not turn my frown around."
"I often wore a smile upside down."
"I was a big disgrace to the human race."
"I very seldom wore a smile on my face."

"I had lost face."
"I was two-faced."
"I could not face life."
"I had egg on my face."

"I had an evil eye."
"I was blind and pie-eyed."
"I could not look one in the eyes."
"I could not see the forest for the trees."

"I was all mouth."
"I had a foul mouth."
"I was mean mouthed."
"I spoke with a forked tongue."

My voice was loud.
"I was ear piercing."
"I stuck my nose in others' business"
and "I was not lean but I was mean."

I was skinny.
"I was a skinflint."
"I was just holding on
by the skin of my teeth."

"I was tightfisted."
"I engaged in fist-a-cuff."
"I was trying to lick the world singlehanded."
"My left hand did not know what my right hand was doing."

I was by no means handsome.
"No one would give me a hand."
"I could not get a grip on myself."
"I could not get a hold on myself."

"I was up in arms."
"I was an elbow bender."
"I did have sticky fingers."
"I was wrapped around a woman's finger."

"I was on my very last leg."
"I did not have a leg to stand on."
"I was brought down to my knees."
"I had weak knees and they knocked."

"I walked the line."
"I had two left feet."
"I was pussyfooting around."
"I could not stand on my own two feet."

"I did have cold feet."
"I could not get a foothold."
"I was footloose and fancy free."
"I constantly stuck my foot in my mouth."

"I was a mental and physical mess from head to toe."
I was not tall and I was quite really oh so small
but then I lifted weights and gave it my all
and then I was so big to be so small.

I was an ass and I was asinine.
I was a horse's behind.
I honestly do tell
all was not so well.

"I was dragging tail."
I had even been in jail
and life was really hell.

I had no health or wealth.
I was totally only into Myself.
I thought of Myself and no one else.
I thought I was beyond help and helpless.
So I looked up to and called out to God for help.

I was lost in sin.
I did not care then.
I was not aware when
I was in slavery to sin then,
when his Son Jesus took me in.

In Christ we all can confide.
In him from the world we can hide.
He conquered all but he did not divide.
He was always straightforward and never lied.
He planted seed that have grown both far and wide.

Far and wide into the hearts of men.
Yet he was marred and scarred by men.
Yes he gave up his life and died for men
because his purpose on the cross was for men.
Christ is the author of eternal salvation for men.

The Lamb overcame and now he is our guide.
And with him and God's speed, we will glide
to go straight to heaven and to be his bride.
And there with God and Jesus we will abide
and we will love them all from deep inside.

And now then at the right of the Greatest of all is my Friend,
the Son of God the Father who loves you all my friend,
the Word of God the Lord of all hosts my friend,
the Lamb of God the Great I a.m. my friend,
What a Friend and More Christ is.
And God is More God is.

God is doing a good work in me,
until the appearing of Jesus you see.
God is making me like I am to be.
I will worship him for eternity you see.

He made me to see when I was blind.
I was looking at his eyes and I did find
in a vision his eyes were kinder than kind.
I nearly cried because his eyes were so kind.

Yes, suddenly God's eyes were there
from out of nowhere.
His eyes were kind and this is true
from out of the blue.

I do not know much
but I do know this.
I'd not seen such
kind eyes as his.

He looked me straight in my eyes.
He looked at me both straight and wide.
His look is enough to make you be true and try.
He straightened out my life and honestly I have not lied.

His eyes were a big surprise.
I did roam far away from home.
But just one look was all it took
to melt my cold hard heart of stone.

He did heal my heart with tenderness.
I had never before seen such kindness.
His eyes were kinder than a holy kiss.
No one had ever looked at me like this.

No one had ever looked at me this way before.
His look went right to my heart's core
and more he had for me in store.
He was certainly no bore.

His eyes did blow my mind.
He broke the shackles that did bind.
He was so kind that he made my heart unwind.
And in my heart and mind no one has ever been so kind.

"The pure in heart shall see God."
"Man seeks the kindness of God."
Amen

Once Upon a Time

Once my life was a mess.
Yes, my life was hell I confess
but he helped me and I was blessed.

Once upon a time
I almost lost my mind
but someone to me was kind.

Once I was down
but then he was around
and he made my mind sound.

Once my heart was not tender
and I was one pretender
but he was for real

and he helped me a great deal.
He filled me with power and zeal
and my mind and heart he did heal.

He healed my mind.
He was gentle and kind
and he treated me just fine.

He healed my broken heart.
He healed me with such art
and he gave me a new start.

He put my feet on solid ground,
although I was hell bent and bound,
and my mind and heart he does astound.

He is the One who took me by the hand.
He is the Son who lived in flesh as man.
He is the One with nail-scarred hands,

who made a stand for God's love to men,
who did come through for men and women
and we do love you, Lord Jesus Christ. Amen.

Once I Was Down

Once Satan got me down
and I was really kicked around.
But then Jesus Christ, he lifted me up
and then he promised with him we will sup.

Once I was down and—out
and I felt I could scream and shout.
But then Jesus Christ the Lord was about
and then he did put a clout on my down and—out.

Once I was sad
and about enough I had had.
But then Jesus spoke to me through my dad
and then he did fill my heart with joy and I was oh so glad.

Once I was as bad as bad could be
and I had not much going for me.
But then Jesus was around you see
and then he taught me how to be.

Once I was as mean as mean could be
and I thought only of Myself you see.
But then Jesus Christ was kind to me
and he turned me around you see.

Now this I can tell,
he treated me well.
I very nearly did sell
my soul for a female.

He bought my soul back for me.
Jesus had mercy on me you see.
He forgave me and blessed me
and welcomed me back you see.

Now please understand,
Jesus with the nail-scarred hands
did make the ultimate sacrifice for men and women.
Yes, he suffered on the cross and he gave up his life for
    men and women.

Now I am telling you
that I believe this is true.
His temple was black and blue
because of all that he went through.

Now try and see
what he means to me.
I do worship the ground on which he walks
and I do love the sound of his voice when he talks.

He is my love, and my life, and my joy.
He has taken care of me since I was a boy.
He has never treated me like I was a play toy
and I will love Jesus for ever after it is ship ahoy.

Jesus lived for God and he died for God
and he does love you, too.
Jesus died for you and he lives for you
and we do love you, too.

Jesus is the Son of God
and the Saviour of men.
Jesus is the Lamb of God,
please look to him. Amen.

Once In a While

Once I was down and—out.
I wondered what life was about.
But now I know without any doubt,
that life is school for you and for me,

so we will all learn how to be.
It starts when we are children you see,
and ends at death, don't you see.
That is when we have learned how to be.

I once was hardheaded
but now I am tenderhearted.
I once was a sinner
but Jesus is a soul winner.

All at once, he was there,
from out of nowhere.
And once Jesus was there,
I was aware he cared.

Once he is there for you
never swear at him.
Once he is there for you
always care for him.

Once he has found you
never let him go.
Once he is around you
always love him so.

Once in a while
shout praise at him.
Once in a while
take a gaze at him.

Once in a while
admire him.
Once in a while
inspire him.

He is once, twice, three times,
†the One for all of us.
He is the One who died one time,
once and for all of us.

He died for God.
He died for us.
He is the Lamb of God.
He is our Friend Jesus.

He is the Lamb of God and the Saviour of men
who once did pay the price for the sins of men.
He is the Son of God who once walked with men
and we do worship you, Lord Jesus Christ. Amen.

Once Is Not Enough

Once is just not enough.
Without him, it is tough.
I must thank him again.
I must praise him again.
I must bray to him again.
I must pray to him again.
I must cry for him again.
I must try for him again.
I must give for him again.
I must live for him again.
I must be near him again.
I must be with him again.
I must talk with him again.
I must walk with him again.
Amen

The Son Is the One

No son you see
is greater than he.
He is the best
out of all the rest.

The Son is the One you can talk with
and Sí He is someone you can reason with.
The Son is the One you can walk with
and Sí He is Someone you can really be with.

The Son is the One you can abide in
and Sí He is Someone you can have faith in.
The Son is the One you can confide in
and Sí He is Someone you can have confidence in.

The Son is the One you can trust in
and Sí He is Someone you can feel safe in.
The Son is the One you can believe in
and Sí He is Someone you can feel secure in.

The Son is the One you can call out to
and Sí He is Someone you can look up to.
The Son is the One you can reach out to
and Sí He is Someone you can always go to.

The Son is the One you can always count on
and Sí He is Someone you can always lean on.
The Son is the One you can one always rely on
and Sí He is Someone you can always depend on.

The Son is the One who can help you
and Sí He is Someone who feels for you.
The Son is the One who can heal you
and Sí He is Someone who is real for you.

The Son is not a carry on or put on
and Sí He is certainly no one to step on.
His strong shoulders you can cry on
and with Jesus you can always hold on.

The Son He cares very much for you all
and Sí He can touch the very heart of you.
The Son is a dream come true for you all
and Sí He can make true the dreams of you.

The Son is the One we all have dreamed of
and of his loving ways we all have heard of.
The Son is the One you are in search of
and Sí He is Someone you are in need of.

The Son He is your and my Friend
and Sí He is for you and me my friend.
The Son He is the One for you my friend
and Sí He is the One you are for my friend.

Oui He is the One for you all, men and women.
Oui He is the One for all of us, men and women.
Oui He is the One for the two of us, you and me.
Oui He is the One with nail-scarred hands you see.

He won the war.
It was us he bled for.
It was our stripes he bore
and it was us that he died for.

The Son is Someone worthy of our praise.
He paid the price for the world's sin
then the Son from the dead God did raise
and we love you, Sweet Jesus. Amen.

One Was the Loneliest Number

God Almighty did send Jesus down to earth
and some 32 years after his special birth,
he filled our hearts with sorrow and mirth.

He cried out, "My God, my God, why hath thou forsaken
    me?"
He cried out that terrible yet wonderful day at Calvary.
And One was the loneliest number at Calvary.

He was the # One Son of God at Calvary.
He obeyed his Father's will at Calvary.
He died a horrible death at Calvary.

He was the # One alone at Calvary.
He was crucified and died at Calvary.
And he suffered until he died at Calvary.

He was the # One of three at Calvary.
He was nailed to the Cross at Calvary.
And with two sinners he died at Calvary.

He gave up his life at Calvary.
He laid down his life at Calvary.
And for sinners he died at Calvary.

He gave it his all at Calvary.
He gave it his all out at Calvary.
And for sinners he took it at Calvary.

He is grand.
He has the upper hand.
And for sinners he made a stand.

He is sin free, my friend.
He is the way to be, my friend.
And for you and me, he is my friend.

He suffered and died for you and me, my friend,
that terrible and terrific day at Calvary, my friend
and we do love you, Sweet Jesus Christ. Amen.

The Lord Was, Can, Has, Will, and Is

He was immaculately conceived.
He was never deceitful or deceived.
By his miracles the blind perceived.
He healed the lame, sick, and diseased,
and suffering and misery was relieved.

He brought back to life the deceased.
He put the weary and worried at ease
and with his very gentle way, it was easy.
He was well known as the Prince of peace
and as John The Baptist's fame did decrease,

the Lord Jesus Christ's fame was on the increase.
He preached the kingdom of God and seldom ceased,
and by him the bound and oppressed were released,
and he was always calm though taunted and teased,
and for lost sinners, he was very sad and bereaved.

In his Son Yahweh was well pleased.
God's mission of salvation he achieved.
By him lost sinners souls were retrieved,
and honor, glory, and power he did receive.
On the Lord Jesus Christ you must believe.

He gave freely to everyone in need.
He traveled about with God's speed
and never showed any sign of greed
and of the Lord legions did take heed.
He brought Satan down to his knees.

He was obedient until death,
down until his very last breath.
He was conqueror of his quest
and he did pass all of his tests.
He gives freely to us his guests

honor, glory, and power that is ours.
He tends to us by the hours.
He possesses all powers.
He can send showers
on the flowers.

Any person he can tame.
He does not play games.
He knows all our names.
He treats us all the same.
He has earned his fame.

He can be your crutch.
He keeps secrets a hush.
He knew no sin or such.
He has a certain touch.
He loves us very much.

He has a certain lure.
He will get you for sure.
His special love is pure,
more love than any fuhrer.
No one has ever been truer.

He has every situation covered like crust
and his judgments are just.
In him you can trust,
make it or bust.
It is a must.

He will turn that city life to country town.
He will turn away the junkyard hound.
He will turn your life around.
He will turn your frown
upside down.

He will buy you.
He will satisfy you.
He will never try you.
He will not deny you.
He will not lie to you.

He will not hurt you.
He will not desert you.
He will not harm you.
He will not alarm you
and he will charm you.

He will not hassle you.
He will razzle you
and he will dazzle you.
He will amaze you
and he will surprise you.

He will care for you indeed.
He will meet your every need.
He may act with lightning speed.
He may act at the speed of light.
For you he did suffer and bleed.

He will sometimes make haste.
He will stick to you like paste.
He may make you chaste.
He does not waste.
He is good taste.

He will fill your life with joy.
He will not treat you like a toy.
He loves the little girls and boys.
He is tolerant of their loud noises
and with him they need not be coy.

He needs no introduction.
He listens to our suggestions.
He will answer all our questions.
He is for you all making preparations.
"In his Father's house are many mansions."

His heart is soft,
as smooth as cloth.
He will never lay you off
and he will never put you off.
His TLC will never ever wear off.

He is no fake.
He does not take.
He will never forsake.
You a star he will make.
Your heart he will never break.

He is an ace.
He gives us grace.
No matter what place,
even in extreme outer space,
he is more protective than mace.

He knows no defeat.
He cannot be beat.
He is really neat.
He is oh so sweet.
Jesus we will meet.
Amen

*I*f You Are in Need, then the Lord Is Ready, Willing, and Able to Help Indeed

If you are unsteady
and you need one not heavy,
then the Lord Jesus Christ, he is ready.

If you are thinking about suicide
or you are not sure or cannot decide,
in the Lord Jesus you will be able to hide.

If suicide is on your mind,
then put the past behind
and Jesus will be kind.

If your mind has been blown
from something you've been shown,
then the Lord he will not let you be alone.

If you are weak
or suffer defeat,
he can be sweet.

If you are weary
or your eyes are teary,
then he can make you merry.

If you cannot sleep
or are about to weep
your soul he will keep.

If you have gone to bed to rest your weary head
and you are not in the red and toss and turn instead,
then he can give you peaceful dreams, it has been said.

If you have made your own miserable bed
or are suffering from something you've said,
the Lord can cure for sure as heavy is lead.

the Lord can make the deaf to hear
or he can cure you from whiskey or beer
and "the Lord he is able to draw all men near."

If you are unable to walk or talk,
the Lord can make the lame to walk
and the Lord can make the dumb to talk.

If you are not very bright
or you cannot even read or write,
all you need know is wrong from right.

If you are going to fast, you might not last.
You indeed do need to take heed of your speed
or to the Lord Jesus Christ you may never proceed.

If you are headstrong,
it won't be long before you are gone.
To the Saviour, the Lord Jesus Christ, you should belong.

If you go through life
and make one Dear Friend,
then you are doing pretty doggone good.

If you go through life
and make Jesus your Friend,
then you are doing as well as you should.

If you cannot cope with life
or you cannot handle the strife,
then you would make Jesus a good wife.

If you have given up hope
or are at the end of your rope,
then he can make you able to cope.

If you smoke or are on dope
or are hopped up and can't stop,
the Lord, he is able to help you a lot.

If you are addicted to a drug or a pill
or you are in search of something real,
the Lord, he is able to give you a thrill.

If you have been had or are mad
or you are feeling bad or you are sad,
the Lord, he is able to make you very glad.

If you have been used and abused
or your troubles seem to come in twos,
the Lord, he is able to soothe and smooth.

If you are in bad trouble
or someone has busted your bubble,
the Lord, he is able to help you on the double.

If at any minute you may go
or you are a wino or are on death row,
the Lord he is able to still love you so, you know.

If you have committed a crime
or you are serving some time,
the Lord can keep you in line.

If you do not have much time
or are cut down in you prime,
the Lord is good as a lifeline.

If you wish you were dead,
then why not think instead
of Jesus to heal your head.

If your days are numbered,
he is once, twice, three times
the One and only One for all of you.

If death is here,
no need to fear,
the Lord is near.

If you have a terribly tormented soul
or are going to die, you have been told,
the Lord, he can make you totally whole.

If you are not very well, or life is hell,
or you are under a spell, or you cannot tell,
the Lord, he has healing power as deep as a well.

If you are not well aware
or all you can do is stare,
the Lord, he will be there.

If you do not even care
or have something rare,
the Lord, he will be there.

If Satan for you sets a snare,
the Lord, can get you out of there
and he can make you aware he cares.

If you are worried about the environment's care,
the Lord, he is able to clear the water and air,
the Lord, he can renew the earth so there.

If you are worried, or have many doubts,
or you are wondering what life is all about,
on Jesus all your problems you can surmount.

If life has really got you down
or your mind and body are not sound,
then let Jesus Christ turn your frown around.

If you have fallen, get back up,
don't give in and don't give up,
he will take you in and lift you up.

If you have done your best
but your best effort was off,
then Christ made up the cost.

If you are not worth a dime
or do not even have the time,
he is richer than a gold mine.

If you are in need
or have mouths to feed,
he will provide for you indeed.

If you do not have it made
or you are scared and afraid,
the Lord, he will come to your aid.

If someone starts with you a fight
and you are afraid or affright,
always do what is right.

If you do not know how to behave
or if you are scared and afraid,
the Lord, he is very brave.

If you do not know what to do,
then trust in the One who is true
and he will help and see you through

If you do not know how to be,
then study the Bible and see,
the Lord, he is the way to be.
Amen

When You Are in Need, then the Lord Can and Will Help Indeed

When life is dull
and there is a lull,
he can be full of fun.

When life gets rough
and you could give up,
the Lord can hang tough.

When life makes a demand,
he will take you by the hand
and Jesus will make a stand.

When life is not worth living
and you are tired of not getting,
Jesus can be generous and giving.

When you are just surviving,
then why not come alive in
the Lord Jesus Christ.

When you are down
and no one can be found,
he can turn your frown around.

When you are really down and—out
and you are about to scream and shout,
the Lord, he can lift you up without doubt.

When it seems your luck has run out
and you could moan and cry and pout,
the Lord, he can aid you without doubt.

When you don't care
and you could swear,
the Lord can be there.

When you are blue
and nothing will do,
he can rescue you.

When you have been used
and you have been abused,
the Lord can be good news.

When you have been wronged
or feel you do not really belong,
he can be good as a love song.

When you are sad
and you do feel bad,
he can make you glad.

When you feel depressed,
there is no need to fret or worry,
the Lord, he can get to you in a hurry.

When you are possessed
or your soul has been hexed,
he can make you feel blessed.

When your brain feels strain
and you are nearly insane,
he can take away pain.

When you feel like running away
or cannot think of anything to say,
Jesus can help to make your day.

When you do have something to say,
then get on your knees and do pray.
It is a good way to start the day.

When you have lost your way,
like a lost alley cat stray.
Go to Jesus and stay

When you have fallen away
or you have gone astray,
you he will not betray.

When you have roamed
far away from home,
you are not alone.

When the world gives you hell
and you really need someone to tell,
then the Lord Jesus Christ can be swell.
Amen

When and Then

When it seems that the world is crumbling around you,
then be aware that he cares.
When it seems that the sky is falling down,
then be aware that he cares.
When it seems that you are down and—out,
then be aware that he cares.
When it seems that you could give up,
then be aware that he cares.
When it seems that there is no hope,
then be aware that he cares.
When it seems that everything you do is wrong,
then be aware that he cares.
When it seems that nothing you do is right,
then be aware that he cares.
When it seems that life is not worth living,
then be aware that he cares.
When it seems that you could end it all,
then be aware that he cares.
No matter when, what, or where,
then be aware that he cares.
Amen

When You Are Then He Is

When you are abandoned,   then his love is abundant.
When you are abnormal,   then he is above normal.
When you are abominable,   then he is laudable.
When you are abortive,   then he is consummated.
When you are abrupt,   then he is deliberate.
When you are absentminded,   then he is alert.
When you are absurd,   then he is sensible.
When you are abusive,   then he is respectful.
When you are accidental,   then he is essential.
When you are addicted,   then he is drug free.
When you are adulterate,   then he is affable.
When you are adventurous,   then he is cautious.
When you are adverse,   then he is advantageous.
When you are afraid,   then he is brave.
When you are aged,   then he is age-old.
When you are aggravated,   then he can appease.
When you are aggressive,   then he is meek.
When you are agitated,   then he can calm.
When you are agnostic,   then he is acknowledged.
When you are ailing,   then he is vigorous.
When you are aimless,   then he has purpose.
When you are alarming,   then he is charming.
When you are an alcoholic,   then he is sober.
When you are all-in,   then he is all-out.
When you are almost,   then he is exact.
When you are alone,   then he is along.
When you are aloof,   then he is about.

When you are amateurish,	then he is masterful.
When you are ambiguous,	then he is explicit.
When you are ambitious,	then he is content.
When you are amiss,	then he is amiable.
When you are amoral,	then he is moral.
When you are angry,	then he is placid.
When you are in anguish,	then he can comfort.
When you are annoyed,	then he can sooth.
When you are antagonistic,	then he is harmonious.
When you are antisocial,	then he is social.
When you are anxious,	then he is at ease.
When you are appalling,	then he is reassuring.
When you are apprehensive,	then he is confident.
When you are argumentative,	then he is appreciative.
When you are arrogant,	then he is humble.
When you are ashamed,	then he can take away the shame.

When you are assaulting,	then he is assertive.
When you are astonished,	then he is astounding
When you are astray,	then he is the way back.
When you are an atheist,	then he is for real.
When you have audacity,	then he has gentility.
When you are average,	then he is above average.
When you are awkward,	then he is agile.
When you are backstabbing,	then he has backbone.
When you are backward,	then he is forward.
When you are bad,	then he does good.
When you are a bad sport,	then he is a good sport.
When you are bad-tempered,	then he is good-tempered.
When you are bald,	then he has a crown of glory for you.

When you are baleful,	then he is beneficent.
When you are a bandit,	then he is bang-up.
When you are bankrupt,	then he is rich.
When you are barbaric,	then he is civilized.
When you are bare,	then he has cover for you.
When you are barefoot,	then he has shoes for you.
When you are barely,	then he is ample.
When you are barren,	then he can make you fertile.
When you are bashful,	then he is dashing.
When you are a bastard,	then he can be Father.
When you are battered,	then he is quick rising.
When you are beastly,	then he is becoming.
When you are beat,	then he is unbeatable.
When you are bedraggled,	then he is like new.
When you are bedridden,	then he is becalming.
When you are befuddled,	then he is clearheaded.
When you are a beggar,	then he is giving.
When you are behind,	then he is ahead.
When you are belittled,	then he can magnify.
When you are belligerent,	then he is benevolent.
When you are below standard,	then he is above standard.
When you are beneath,	then he is above.
When you are beyond help,	then he can help.
When you are biased,	then he is unbiased.
When you are big headed,	then he is tremendous.
When you are a bigot,	then he is impartial.
When you are a big shot,	then he is big time.
When you are bitchy,	then he is benign.
When you are bitter,	then he is sweet.
When you are a blabbermouth,	then he keeps secrets.

When you are blameful,	then he is blameless.
When you are blasphemous,	then he is redeemer.
When you are blind,	then he is watchful.
When you are blood thirsty,	then he was blood stained.
When you are blue,	then he may be sad, too
When you are blunt,	then he is subtle.
When you are boastful,	then he is modest.
When you are boldfaced,	then he is bold hearted.
When you are a bookie,	then he is a winner.
When you are a bootlicker,	then he stands tall.
When you are boring,	then he is interesting.
When you are bossy,	then he was a servant.
When you are bothersome,	then he is brotherly.
When you are bottomed out,	then he is tops.
When you are brainless,	then he as brainpower.
When you are breathless,	then he can take your breath away, too.
When you are brokenhearted,	then he can heal your broken heart.
When you are brought down,	then he can bring you about.
When you are a bully,	then he can be bullheaded.
When you are a bum,	then he can be your chum.
When you are burdened,	then he can lighten the load.
When you are a busybody,	then he is concerned about you.
When you are cabalistic,	then he is candid.
When you are calamitous,	then he is calculating.
When you are a call girl,	then hang it up and call on Jesus.
When you are callous,	then he is compassionate.

When you are cannibalistic,	then digest the Word of God.
When you cannot,	then he can.
When you are capricious,	then he is staunch.
When you are a captive,	then he is captivating.
When you are careless,	then he is careful.
When you are a carry on,	then he is a carry through.
When you are a castaway,	then he is catching.
When you are ceaseless,	then he is enduring, everlasting, and forever.
When you are a challenge,	then he is champion.
When you are changeable,	then he is then now and to be, he is the same.
When you are chaotic,	then he can take charge.
When you are characterless,	then he has character.
When you are cheap,	then he shows charity.
When you are cheerless,	then he can cheer you up.
When you deal in chicanery,	then he is chivalrous.
When you are childish,	then he is a grown-up.
When you are choosy,	then he is choice.
When you are a chump,	then he can be a chum.
When you are circumstantial,	then he is circumspect.
When you are clamorous,	then he is civil.
When you are back class,	then he is classy.
When you are closed-hearted,	then he is open-hearted.
When you are closed-minded,	then he is open-minded.
When you are cloudy,	then he is clear.
When you are clumsy,	then he is graceful.
When you are coarse,	then he is fine.
When you are cold,	then he is warm and cool.
When you are cold-blooded,	then he is warm-blooded.

When you are cold-hearted,   then he is warm-hearted.
When you are cold-shouldered, then he is in no sweat.
When you are collusive,   then he is collected.
When you are colorless,   then he is colorful.
When you are comatose,   then he is wide awake.
When you are come-off,   then he is come-on.
When you are comfortless,   then he is a comfort.
When you are committed,   then he is committed to his.
When you are common,   then he is noble.
When you are common law,   then he is strictly law.
When you need company,   then he is a companion.
When you are compassionless,   then he is compassionate.
When you are a complainer,   then he never complained.
When you are complicated,   then he can be simple.
When you have lost composure, then he is composed.
When you are conceited,   then he is confident.
When you are condemned,   then he was also.
When you lack confidence,   then he has confidence.
When you are a con man,   then he is the confident
                                 Son of man.

When you are confused,   then he is clear headed.
When you are conniving,   then he is conscientious.
When you are conquered,   then he is unconquerable.
When you are a conspirator,   then he is inspirational.
When you are contagious,   then he is catching.
When you are contaminated,   then he can purify.
When you are contemptible,   then he is admirable.
When you are contentious,   then he is courteous.
When you are continuous,   then he is discontinuous.
When you are contradictive,   then he may contravene.
When you are contrary,   then he is the opposite.

When you are controversial,	then he is convincing.
When you are a convict,	then "he bore stripes for you."
When you are corrupt,	then he is incorruptible.
When you are counterfeit,	then he is genuine.
When you are covert,	then he is candid.
When you are covetous,	then he does not want.
When you are cowardly,	then he is courageous.
When you are crabby,	then he is not cranky.
When you are crazy,	then he is sane.
When you are a creep,	then he is steep.
When you are you are a criminal,	then he has committed no crime.
When you are critical,	then throw no stones.
When you are crooked,	then he is straight.
When you are at a crossroad,	then look to the Cross.
When you are cruel,	then he is kind.
When you are crying,	then cry on his shoulder.
When you are curious,	then he is cautious.
When you curse,	then he never cursed.
When you are cursed,	then he has never cursed you.
When you have been cut down,	then he can build you up.
When you are a cut up,	then cut it out.
When you are cynical,	then he is hopeful.
When you are damaging,	then he can repair.
When you are damned,	then he can bless you.
When you are dangerous,	then he is safe.
When you are daring,	then he is dashing.
When you are in darkness,	then he is the Light.

When you are a daydreamer,	then he is a dream come true.
When you are near death,	then "he is vital."
When you are deathly,	then he is lively.
When you are a dealer,	then he makes no deals.
When you are debased,	then he can elevate you.
When you are debauch,	then he is debonair.
When you are in debt,	then he is well off.
When you are deceitful,	then he is not devious.
When you are in deep water,	then he is deep rooted.
When you are defaced,	then he is not default.
When you are defamed,	then he is not default.
When you are defeated,	then he is undefeated.
When you are defenseless,	then he can defend you.
When you are deficient,	then he is efficient.
When you are defiled,	then he is pure.
When you are deformed,	then he can reform you.
When you are defrauded,	then he can defray you.
When you are a degenerate,	then he can regenerate you.
When you are degraded,	then he can upgrade you.
When you are dejected,	then he can exhilarate you.
When you are delicate,	then he is delighted.
When you are delirious,	then he is deliverer.
When you are demanding,	then he is commanding.
When you are demented,	then he is tolerant.
When you are demonic,	then he is above the angels.
When you are demoralized,	then he is uplifting.
When you are dense,	then he is sparse.
When you are deplorable,	then he is irreplaceable.
When you are depraved,	then he is craved.

When you are depressed,	then he can make you bloom.
When you are desolate,	then he can inhabit.
When you are destructive,	then he is constructive.
When you are detestable,	then he is adorable.
When you are devilish,	then he is Lord.
When you are devious,	then he is straightforward.
When you are a dictator,	then he is in command.
When you dilly,	then he does not dally.
When you are dim,	then he is bright.
When you are dirty,	then he is clean.
When you are discouraged,	then he is encouraging.
When you are discourteous,	then he is courteous.
When you are discreditable,	then he is incredible.
When you are discriminatory,	then he is indiscriminatory.
When you are diseased,	then he is the cure-all.
When you are disenchanted,	then he is enchanting.
When you are dishonest,	then he is honest.
When you are dishonorable,	then he is honorable.
When you are disliked,	then he is liked.
When you are disloyal,	then he is loyal.
When you are disobedient,	then he is obedient.
When you are disorderly,	then he is orderly.
When you are dispirited,	then he is spirited.
When you are displeasing,	then he is pleasing.
When you are disregarded,	then he is regarded.
When you are disreputable,	then he is reputable.
When you are disrespectful,	then he is respectful.
When you are disruptive,	then he is orderly.
When you are dissuasive,	then he is persuasive.
When you are distant,	then he is near.

When you are distasteful,	then he has taste.
When you are distressed,	then he can stand the stress.
When you distrustful,	then he is trustful.
When you are divorced,	then he is unmarried.
When you are domineering,	then he is dominant.
When you are doomed,	then he can help.
When you are double-faced,	then he is of one face.
When you are double-minded,	then he is of one mind.
When you are in doubt,	then he is sure.
When you are a downcast,	then he was also.
When you are downhearted,	then he can lift you up.
When you are downtrodden,	then he can lift you up.
When you are drowning,	then he walked on water.
When you are dubious,	then he is trustworthy.
When you are dull,	then he is smart.
When you are earthly,	then he is heavenly.
When you are eccentric,	then he is moral.
When you are effeminate,	then he is masculine.
When you are egocentric,	then he is concerned of others.
When you are elusive,	then he is not evasive.
When you are enabled,	then he is able.
When you are endless,	then he is infinite.
When you are enormous,	then he is enough.
When you are enslaved,	then he can set you free.
When you are entrapped,	then he can set you free.
When you are envious,	then he is not green.
When you are erratic,	then he is stable.
When you are in error,	then he is correct.
When you are evil,	then he is holy.
When you exaggerate,	then he is exact.

When you are excessive,	then he is necessary.
When you are exhausted,	then he has strength.
When you are extravagant,	then he is moderate.
When you are extreme,	then he is supreme.
When you are a failure,	then he is success.
When you are fair,	then he is fabulous.
When you are faithless,	then he is faithful.
When you are a fake,	then he is no phony.
When you are fallible,	then he is infallible.
When you are false,	then he is true.
When you are not famous,	then he is famous.
When you are fat,	then rearrange and change your diet and pray.
When you are fatherless,	then he can be father.
When you are fatigued,	then he is energetic.
When you are faulty,	then he is flawless.
When you are fearful,	then he is fearless.
When you are feeble-minded,	then he is decisive.
When you are a fiend,	then he is our Friend.
When you are fighter,	then he is peacemaker.
When you are filthy,	then he is clean.
When you are finicky,	then he is fine.
When you are fishy,	then he is first rate.
When you are flagrant,	then he is not shocking.
When you are flaky,	then he is together.
When you are flesh,	then he is spirit.
When you are flighty,	then he is firm.
When you are flippant,	then he is serious.
When you are foggy,	then he is clear.
When you are a follower,	then follow him.
When you are foolish,	then he is wise.

When you are forceful,	then he is more forceful.
When you are forward,	then he is not forward.
When you are foul-mouthed,	then he is silver tongued.
When you are fractious,	then he is fractured.
When you are frail,	then he is strong.
When you are frantic,	then he is controlled.
When you are freakish,	then he is normal.
When you are a freeloader,	then he gives freely.
When you are fretful,	then he is not worried.
When you are friendless,	then he is friendly.
When you are frightful,	then he is frightless.
When you are frivolous,	then he is serious.
When you are fruitless,	then he is fruitful.
When you are frustrated,	then he is not flustered.
When you are a fugitive,	then he is forgiving.
When you are furious,	then he is calm.
When you are fussy,	then he is not cussy.
When you have all the gall,	then he is gallant.
When you are a gambler,	then take a chance on Christ.
When you are gaudy,	then he has taste.
When you are gawky,	then he is gainly.
When you are gay,	then there is a better way.
When you are ghostly,	then he can make you Ghostly.
When you are gloomy,	then he can make you sunny.
When you are gluttonous,	then don't be pigheaded.
When you are Godforsaken,	then maybe Christ can help.
When you are Godless,	then he is Godlike.
When you are a goldbricker,	then he is as good as gold.

When you are goofy,	then he is no dunce.
When you are a gossip,	then he is tightlipped.
When you are graceless,	then he is graceful.
When you are greedy,	then be only needy.
When you are grief-stricken,	then he is a comfort.
When you are grotesque,	then he can cure you.
When you are grouchy,	then he is unirritated.
When you are grumpy,	then he is good tempered.
When you are guileful,	then he is guileless.
When you are guilty,	then he is guiltless.
When you are habitual,	then he is habit forming.
When you are half-hearted,	then he is whole hearted.
When you are a half-wit,	then he is witty.
When you are handicapped,	then he does handiwork.
When you are hung over,	then you should hang it up.
When you are hard-boiled,	then he is hard-core.
When you are hardheaded,	then he can be hard-shelled.
When you are harebrained,	then he is harmonious.
When you are harmful,	then he is harmless.
When you are harsh,	then he is not rough.
When you are hateful,	then he is loving.
When you are haughty,	then he is neither haughty nor naughty.

When you are headstrong,	then he is not stiff necked.
When you are hearing voices,	then listen for Sweet Jesus.
When you are heartless,	then he is hearty.
When you are a heathen,	then he is Godlike.
When you are heavy-handed,	then he is light handed.
When you are heavy-hearted,	then he is light hearted.
When you are a heckler,	then heck, you need Jesus.
When you are heedless,	then he is heedful.

When you are a heel,	then he may put his foot down.
When you are hell,	then he is heaven.
When you are a hellcat,	then you may be hell bent.
When you are helpless,	then he is helpful.
When you are a heretic,	then he is the gospel.
When you are a hermit,	then he is outgoing.
When you are hesitant,	then he is onward.
When you are hideous,	then hide in him.
When you are high-handed,	then he is high born.
When you are high-minded,	then he is high priest.
When you are high-strung,	then he is high spirited.
When you are a hit man,	then he was hit for you.
When you are hollow,	then he is Holy.
When you are homeless,	then he is home base.
When you are homely,	then he was not desirable either.
When you are homesick,	then it will not be long.
When you are homicidal,	then he died for you.
When you are homosexual,	then there is a better way.
When you are a hooker,	then hang it up.
When you are hopeless,	then he is hopeful.
When you are hostile,	then he is hospitable.
When you are hot-headed,	then he is cool.
When you are a huffy,	then he is humble.
When you are human,	then he is spirit.
When you are humiliated,	then he is humane.
When you are humorless,	then he is humorous.
When you are hungry,	then he has food for you.
When you are hunted,	then hunt for him.
When you are hurried,	then he is not worried.

When you are hurt,	then he can heal you.
When you are hurtful,	then he is harmless.
When you are hussy,	then he can be fussy.
When you are hustler,	then hustle to him.
When you are hypnotized,	then he can mesmerize.
When you are a hypocrite,	then take the beam out of your own eye.
When you are an idiot,	then he is ideal.
When you are ignorant,	then he will not ignore you
When you are ill,	then he can heal you.
When you are ill humored,	then he is humorous.
When you are illegal,	then he is legal.
When you are illegitimate,	then he is legitimate.
When you are illiterate,	then he is literate.
When you are ill mannered,	then he is well mannered.
When you are ill natured,	then he is good natured.
When you are illogical,	then he is logical.
When you are ill-spoken of,	then is well spoken of.
When you are ill-tempered,	then he is good tempered.
When you are illusive,	then he is illustrious.
When you are an imbecile,	then imitate him.
When you are immature,	then he is mature.
When you are immobile,	then he is mobile.
When you are immodest,	then he is modest.
When you are immoral,	then he is moral.
When you are impaired,	then he can repair.
When you are impatient,	then he is patient.
When you are impeached,	then he is impeccable.
When you are imperfect,	then he is perfect.
When you are impersonal,	then he is personal.
When you are impertinent,	then he is pertinent.

When you are impetuous,	then he is petuous.
When you are impious,	then he is not impish.
When you are impolite,	then he is polite.
When you are imposing,	then he is reserved.
When you are impossible,	then with him all things are possible.
When you are an imposter,	then he is real.
When you are impotent,	then he can make you potent.
When you are impoverished,	then he is rich.
When you are impractical,	then he is practical.
When you are impressionable,	then he is impressive.
When you are imprisoned,	then he can set you free.
When you are improper,	then he is proper.
When you are improvident,	then he is provident.
When you are imprudent,	then he is prudent.
When you are impulsive,	then he is compulsive.
When you are impure,	then he is pure.
When you are inaccessible,	then he is accessible.
When you are inaccurate,	then he is accurate.
When you are inactive,	then he is active.
When you are inadequate,	then he is adequate.
When you are inadvisable,	then he is advisable.
When you are inappreciable,	then he is appreciable.
When you are inappropriate,	then he is appropriate.
When you are inapt,	then he is apt.
When you are inarticulate,	then he is articulate.
When you are inattentive,	then he is attentive.
When you are inauspicious,	then he is auspicious.
When you are incapable,	then he is capable.
When you are incarcerated,	then he can set you free.

When you are incautious,	then he is cautious.
When you are incestuous,	then he is angry.
When you are uncivil,	then he is civil.
When you are incoherent,	then he is coherent.
When you are incommunicable,	then he is communicable.
When you are incompatible,	then he is compatible.
When you are incompetent,	then he is competent.
When you are incomplete,	then he is complete.
When you are incomprehensible,	then he is comprehensible.
When you are inconsiderate,	then he is considerate.
When you are inconsistent,	then he is consistent.
When you are incorrect,	then he is correct.
When you are incorrigible,	then he is incorruptible.
When you are incriminated,	then who is fit to judge?
When you are incurable,	then he can cure you.
When you are indebted,	then he paid the debt.
When you are indecisive,	then he is decisive.
When you are indefinite,	then he is definite.
When you are indifferent,	then he makes the difference.
When you are indigent,	then he can provide.
When you are indignant,	then he is dignant.
When you are indirect,	then he is direct.
When you are indiscrete,	then he is discrete.
When you are indolent,	then he is dolent.
When you are inebriated,	then he stayed sober.
When you are ineffective,	then he is effective.
When you are inefficient,	then he is efficient and beneficent.
When you are inelegant,	then he is elegant.
When you are inept,	then he is able.

When you are inexact,	then he is exact.
When you are inexpedient,	then he is expedient.
When you are inexperienced,	then he is experienced.
When you are inexplicit,	then he is explicit.
When you are inexpressive,	then he is expressive.
When you are infantile,	then he is grown-up.
When you are inferior,	then he is superior.
When you are an infidel,	then he is vital.
When you are infirm,	then he is firm.
When you are inglorious,	then he is glorious.
When you are an ingrate,	then he is grateful.
When you are inharmonious,	then he is harmonious.
When you are inhospitable,	then he is hospitable.
When you are inhumane,	then he is humane.
When you are iniquitous,	then he is indulgent.
When you are injurious,	then he is not harmful.
When you are an inmate,	then he can set you free.
When you are an inpatient,	then he is patient.
When you are insane,	then he is sane.
When you are inscrutable,	then he is easily understood.
When you are insensible,	then he is sensible.
When you are insensitive,	then he is sensitive.
When you are insidious,	then he is sidious.
When you are insignificant,	then he is significant.
When you are insincere,	then he is sincere.
When you are insipid,	then he is sipid.
When you are insolent,	then he is solent.
When you are an instigator,	then he is a navigator.
When you are institutionalized,	then he can be there to care.
When you are insubordinate,	then he is subordinate.

When you are insufficient,   then he is sufficient.
When you are insulting,   then he is not rude.
When you are intemperate,   then he is temperate.
When you are interracial,   then it is all right.
When you are intimidated,   then he is unintimidated.
When you are intolerant,   then he is tolerant.
When you are intoxicated,   then he is sober.
When you are an introvert,   then he is an extrovert.
When you are an invalid,   then he is valid.
When you are involuntary,   then he is voluntary.
When you are irrational,   then he is rational.
When you are irregular,   then he can make you
                                 regular.

When you are irreligious,   then he is religion.
When you are irrespectful,   then he is respectful.
When you are irresponsible,   then he is responsible.
When you are irreverent,   then he is reverent.
When you are irritable,   then he calmed stormy
                                 waters.

When you are isolated,   then he can be there.
When you are a jackass,   then kick the habit.
When you are a jailbird,   then sing to Jesus.
When you are jealous,   then he is zealous.
When you are a jerk,   then don't jive.
When you are joyless,   then he can make you
                                 joyful.

When you are jumpy,   then he can make you
                                 jubilant.

When you are juvenile,   then he is grown-up.
When you are a kibitzer,   then he has advice for you.
When you are kidnapped,   then he is ransom enough.

When you are a killer,	then he was killed for you.
When you are a killjoy,	then live and let live.
When you are kinky,	then get straight.
When you are a Klansman,	then he has a plan for you.
When you are a know-nothing,	then he is knowledgeable.
When you are laborious,	then he can give you rest.
When you are lacerated,	then he can heal you.
When you are lame,	then he can heal you.
When you are languished,	then he is strong.
When you are late,	then he is on time.
When you are a lawbreaker,	then he is law abiding.
When you are lawless,	then he is lawful.
When you are lazy,	then he is a worker.
When you are a leach,	then let loose.
When you are least,	then he is the Most.
When you are a lemon,	then he is peachy.
When you are less,	then he is more.
When you are a liar,	then he is truthful.
When you are lifeless,	then he is lively.
When you are light-minded,	then he is serious-minded.
When you are limited,	then he is limitless.
When you are little known,	then he is well-known.
When you are a loafer,	then he is a worker.
When you are loathsome,	then he is wholesome.
When you are lofty,	then get down with Jesus.
When you are lonely,	then you are not alone.
When you are a long shot,	then he is long suffering.
When you are a loser,	then he is a winner.
When you are a loud mouth,	then he is soft spoken.
When you are loveless,	then he is loveable.
When you are low-spirited,	then he can raise your spirit.

When you are luckless,	then he is lucky.
When you are a lunatic,	then he is sane.
When you are a lush,	then he is sober.
When you are lustful,	then he is not.
When you are mad,	then he may be sad.
When you are in the Mafia,	then he can do magic.
When you are maimed,	then he is miraculous.
When you are maladjusted,	then he is adjusted.
When you are malevolent,	then he is magnificent.
When you are malicious,	then he does not malign.
When you are malnourished,	then he has nutrition for you.
When you are malpracticing,	then stop.
When you are a man,	then overcome and become a son of God.
When you are a man-eater,	then digest the Word of God.
When you are a man-handler,	then he can handle you.
When you are a maniac,	then he is sane.
When you are marred,	then he can heal scars.
When you are marooned,	then he can be there.
When you are a masochist,	then he took the pain for you.
When you are a matador,	then bull.
When you are a matchmaker,	then he is master.
When you are a materialist,	then he is spiritualist.
When you are mealy-mouthed,	then he is silver-tongued.
When you are mean,	then he is kind.
When you are meaningless,	then he is meaningful.
When you are meddlesome,	then he is measureless.
When you are melancholy,	then he is melodious.

When you are a menace,	then be like Christ, not Dennis.
When you are mentally deficient,	then he is mentally sufficient.
When you are merciless,	then he is merciful.
When you are merely,	then he is severely.
When you are a mess,	then he is tidy.
When you have a migraine,	then he can sooth.
When you are militant,	then he is nonmilitant.
When you are mindless,	then he is mindful.
When you are minor,	then he is major.
When you are minus,	then he is plus.
When you are mirthless,	then he is mirthful.
When you are misapprehended,	then he is apprehended.
When you misbehave,	then he behaves
When you miscarry,	then he can carry you.
When you are mischievous,	then he is not.
When you are misdirected,	then he can redirect you.
When you are a miser,	then he is giving.
When you are a misfit,	then he is fitting.
When you are misfortunate,	then he is fortunate.
When you are misguided,	then he can guide you.
When you are misinformed,	then he is well informed.
When you are misinterpreted,	then he is not misconstrued.
When you are misjudged,	then he is judge.
When you are misled,	then he can lead you.
When you mismanage,	then he can manage.
When you misplace,	then he can replace.
When you misremember,	then he remembers.
When you misrepresent,	then he can represent.

When you are missing,	then he can find you.
When you are mistaken,	then he is right.
When you mistrust,	then he is trustworthy.
When you are misunderstood,	then he is understanding.
When you are mixed up,	then he can straighten you out.
When you are a mobster,	then he is your model.
When you molest,	then he detests.
When you are monotonous,	then he is magnanimous.
When you are a monster,	then he is not monstrous.
When you are a mooch,	then he can motivate you.
When you are moody,	then he is moony.
When you are morbid,	then he is wholesome.
When you are mortal,	then he is immortal.
When you are mortified,	then he is not morbid.
When you are motionless,	then he can put you in motion.
When you are mournful,	then he may be, too.
When you are mousy,	then he has courage.
When you are muddle-headed,	then he is clear-headed.
When you are murderous,	then he is peaceful.
When you are mute,	then he gives a hoot.
When you are naked,	then he has clothes for you.
When you are nameless,	then he is namable.
When you are narrow-minded,	then he is broad-minded.
When you are nasty,	then he is clean.
When you are naughty,	then he is nice.
When you are nauseating,	then he is not.
When you are nauseous,	then he can sooth.
When you are near-sighted,	then he can see forever.
When you are needy,	then he can meet your need.

When you are negative,   then he is positive.
When you are negligent,   then he is necessary.
When you are nerveless,   then he has nerve.
When you are nerve-racking,   then he is nerve-calming.
When you are nervous,   then he has nerves of steel.
When you are nervy,   then he is never.
When you are neurotic,   then he is sane.
When you have nightmares,   then he can give you peace
                                 of mind.

When you are a nobody,   then he is a somebody.
When you are noisy,   then he is sound.
When you are nonobservant,   then he is observant.
When you are nonreligious,   then he is religion.
When you are nonspiritual,   then he is spiritual.
When you are nonsympathetic,   then he is sympathetic.
When you are nosy,   then he is notable.
When you are nothing,   then he is something.
When you are nowhere,   then he is somewhere.
When you are nude,   then he has clothing for
                                 you.

When you are a nuisance,   then he is helpful.
When you are a numbskull,   then he is a brainstorm.
When you are nutty,   then he can be your buddy.
When you are obese,   then rearrange and change
                                 your diet and pray.

When you are objectionable,   then he may object.
When you are oblique,   then he is clear.
When you are oblivious,   then he is aware.
When you are obnoxious,   then he is pious.
When you are obscure,   then he is lucid.
When you are odd,   then he is even.

When you are odious,	then he is not horrid.
When you are off-beat,	then he is on-beat.
When you are offensive,	then he is offenseless.
When you are old,	then he is 33 and ages.
When you are one-sided,	then he is one-way.
When you are oppressed,	then he can set you free.
When you are ornery,	then he is not mean.
When you are an orphan,	then he can be Father.
When you are an outcast,	then he is outgoing.
When you are an outpatient,	then he is outreaching.
When you are outrageous,	then he is outraged.
When you are overactive,	then he is active.
When you are overanxious,	then he can calm.
When you are overbearing,	then he is forbearing.
When you are overboard,	then he is above board.
When you are overcome,	then he has overcome.
When you are overconfident,	then he is confident.
When you are overweight,	then rearrange and change your diet and pray.
When you owe,	then he owns.
When you are pagan,	then he is pious.
When you are painful,	then he feels the pain.
When you are painted,	then he is colorful.
When you are a palmist,	then his were Nail-Scarred.
When you are panicky,	then he is calm.
When you are paranoid,	then he is not afraid.
When you are particular,	then he is perfect.
When you are part-time,	then he is full-time.
When you are passive,	then he is compassionate.
When you are a pauper,	then he is rich.
When you are peculiar,	then he is perfect.

When you are peevish,	then he is full-time.
When you are penniless,	then he is penny-wise.
When you are perfidious,	then he is a perfectionist.
When you are perplexed,	then he is persistent.
When you are persecuted,	then so was he.
When you are persuadable,	then he is persuasive.
When you are perverse,	then he is incorruptible.
When you are pessimistic,	then he is optimistic.
When you are pettish,	then he is not irritable.
When you are petulant,	then he is not irritable.
When you are a philanderer,	then he is serious.
When you are philosophical,	then he is Biblical.
When you are phony,	then he is real.
When you are physical,	then he is spiritual.
When you are picky,	then pick Christ.
When you are a pimp,	then he is no imp.
When you are in the pits,	then he is top notch.
When you are pitiful,	then he is piteous.
When you are plastic,	then he is steel.
When you are a playboy,	then he does not play around.
When you are plump,	then fast and pray.
When you are pointless,	then he is poignant.
When you are pokey,	then he is not hokey.
When you are political,	then he is nonpartisan.
When you pollute,	then he gives a hoot.
When you are a polygamist,	then be monogamist.
When you are pompous,	then he is not arrogant.
When you are in the poor house,	then he is in a mansion of yours.
When you are possessed,	then he can exorcise you.

When you are possessive, then he possesses all.
When you are potbellied, then fast and pray.
When you are poverty stricken, then he is rich.
When you are powerless, then he is powerful.
When you are a prankster, then he never pulls pranks.
When you are precarious, then he is precautionary.
When you are prejudice, then he is unprejudiced.
When you are preposterous, then he is not absurd.
When you are presumptuous, then he is not brash.
When you are pretentious, then he is unpretentious.
When you are prideful, then he is priestly.
When you are primitive, then he is modern.
When you are a prisoner, then he can pardon you.
When you are a prissy, then he is no sissy.
When you are a prodigal, then he can make you prosper.

When you are profane, then he is not obscene.
When you are promiscuous, then he is prudent.
When you are a prostitute, then "sin no more."
When you are proud, then he resists you.
When you are provoking, then he does not harass.
When you are psycho, then he is psychic.
When you are psychosomatic, then he can give you psychotherapy.

When you are punchy, then he did not fight.
When you are puny, then he is wholesome.
When you are purposeless, then he is purposeful.
When you are pushy, then he is not offensive.
When you are put down, then he can lift you up.
When you are a put on, then he can put you out.
When you are putrid, then he is poised.

When you are quarrelsome,	then he is peaceful.
When you are queer,	then there is a better way.
When you are questionable,	then he is unquestionable.
When you are a rabble rouser,	then he is a pacifist.
When you are a racist,	then he is nonracial.
When you are a racketeer,	then he can be radical.
When you are railroaded,	then he can carry the baggage.
When you are raped,	then his help can be rapid.
When you are rattlebrained,	then he is reasonable.
When you are rebellious,	then he is obedient.
When you are reckless,	then he is cautious.
When you are redundant,	then he is not repetitious.
When you are regardless,	then he is regardful.
When you are regressive,	then he is progressive.
When you are regretful,	then he can make you forget.
When you are relentless,	then he is persistent.
When you are reluctant,	then he is remarkable.
When you are remorseless,	then he is remorseful.
When you are repulsive,	then he is respected.
When you are resistless,	then he is irresistible.
When you are restless,	then he is restful.
When you are retarded,	then he is respondent.
When you are revengeful,	then vengeance is his.
When you are reviled,	then so was he.
When you are revolting,	then he is righteous.
When you are rich,	then he gives.
When you are ridiculous,	then he is rigorous.
When you are a ringleader,	then he is your rival.
When you are rootless,	then he has heavenly roots.

When you are rough,	then he is gentle.
When you are ruff,	then he is ready.
When you are ruffled,	then he is unruffled.
When you are a runaway,	then he can be home.
When you are ruthless,	then he is merciful.
When you are sacrilegious,	then he is sacred.
When you are sad,	then he is not glad.
When you are sadistic,	then he is sanctified.
When you are sarcastic,	then he is not sardonic.
When you are sassy,	then he does not take back talk.
When you are satanic,	then he is saintly.
When you are a savage,	then he is savant.
When you are a scalawag,	then he is not scandalous.
When you are scared,	then he is brave.
When you are scatterbrained,	then he is together.
When you are scheming,	then he is not conniving.
When you are schizophrenic,	then he is single-minded.
When you are scornful,	then he is respectful.
When you are scrappy,	then he never scuffled.
When you are seclusive,	then he is not secluded.
When you are second class,	then he is first class.
When you play second fiddle,	then he plays first fiddle.
When you are second rate,	then he is first rate.
When you are second string,	then he is first string.
When you are secular,	then he is sacred.
When you are seductive,	then he is sedulous.
When you are a segregationist,	then he is an integrationist.
When you are self-centered,	then he is self-assured.
When you are self-conscious,	then he is self-confident.
When you are self-destructive,	then he is self-controlled.

When you are selfish,	then he is unselfish.
When you are self-righteous,	then he is self-disciplined.
When you are semiconscious,	then he is conscious of you.
When you are senile,	then he is sensational.
When you are senseless,	then he is sensible.
When you are a serf,	then he is a servant.
When you are setback,	then he is not slack.
When you are a sexist,	then he is not sexual.
When you are shady,	then he is sunny.
When you are shaky,	then he is still.
When you are shiftless,	then he is not shifty.
When you are shocking,	then he is electrifying.
When you are shortsighted,	then he is second sighted.
When you are a show-off,	then he is not showy.
When you are a shut-in,	then let Jesus in.
When you are shy,	then he is bold.
When you are sick,	then he can heal for real.
When you are sightless,	then he is sightly.
When you are silly,	then he is serious.
When you are sinful,	then he is sinless.
When you are sinister,	then he never sinned.
When you are a sissy,	then he is not prissy.
When you are a skeptic,	then don't be a doubting Thomas.
When you are on skid row,	then he can put you on the front row.
When you are a skinflint,	then he is matchless.
When you are a slave,	then he is an abolitionist.
When you are a slob,	then he is tidy.
When you are sloppy,	then he is neat.
When you are slothful,	then he is not lazy.

When you are a sluggard,   then consider the ant.

When you are sluggish,   then he is energetic.

When you are a slut,   then he can get you out of the rut.

When you are sly,   then he is not wily.

When you are small-minded,   then he is big-minded.

When you are small-time,   then he is big-time.

When you are smelly,   then he is not offensive.

When you are a smoker,   then he is a nonsmoker.

When you are snared,   then he can snatch you out.

When you are sneaky,   then he is not shifty.

When you are snobbish,   then he is not snooty.

When you are a so and so,   then he is not so-so.

When you are soft-headed,   then he can be hardheaded.

When you are a soldier,   then be a Christian soldier.

When you are sometimes,   then he is always.

When you are songless,   then he is songful.

When you are sorrowful,   then he may feel sorrow for you.

When you are soulless,   then he is soulful.

When you are spaced out,   then he is spatial.

When you are spastic,   then he is special.

When you are a spectacle,   then he is spectacular.

When you are speechless,   then he is the Word of God.

When you are spellbound,   then he can break the spell.

When you are a spendthrift,   then he is thrifty.

When you are spineless,   then he has backbone.

When you are spiritless,   then he is spirited.

When you are spiteful,   then he has no spite.

When you have a split personality, then he is splendid.

When you are a spoilsport,	then he is the life of the party.
When you are a sponge,	then dry out.
When you are spooky,	then he is spunky.
When you are square,	then he is triune.
When you are squeamish,	then he has a strong stomach.
When you are at a stalemate,	then he is a checkmate.
When you are starry-eyed,	then he achieved stardom.
When you are sterile,	then he can make you virile.
When you are a stinker,	then he is not sticky.
When you are stir crazy,	then he is stirring.
When you are strange,	then he is not weird.
When you are a striker,	then he never struck.
When you are stubborn,	then be a stubborn Christian.
When you are stupid,	then he is brilliant.
When you are substandard,	then he is substantial.
When you are subversive,	then he is not adversative.
When you are suffering,	then he is longsuffering.
When you are suicidal,	then he is suitable.
When you are sulky,	then he is super.
When you are sullen,	then he is superb.
When you are sunless,	then he is sunny.
When you are superstitious,	then he is supernatural.
When you are suppressed,	then he is supreme.
When you are surly,	then he is not sullen.
When you are suspicious,	then he knows.
When you are tacky,	then he is classy.
When you are tactless,	then he is tactful.
When you are in a tailspin,	then he can pull you out.

When you are toneless,	then he is tone.
When you are tardy,	then he is never truant.
When you are tasteless,	then he is tasteful.
When you are taunting,	then he is not teasing.
When you are tearful,	then he can make you cheerful
When you are tempestuous,	then he is tempered.
When you are tempted,	then he resisted.
When you are tempting,	then he is tempted.
When you are terminal,	then he is long lasting.
When you are terrible,	then he is terrific.
When you are tested,	then he is triumphant.
When you are testy,	then he has been tested.
When you are thankless,	then he is thankful.
When you are thick-headed,	then he is not thick-witted.
When you are thick-witted,	then he is clever.
When you are a thief,	then you could steal go blind.
When you are third class,	then he is first class.
When you are third rate,	then he is first rate.
When you are thirsty,	then he is living water.
When you are thoughtless,	then he is thoughtful.
When you are threatening,	then he is not threatened.
When you are thriftless,	then he is thrifty.
When you are ticked off,	then he may be angry, too.
When you are a tightwad,	then he gives freely.
When you are timid,	then he is courageous.
When you are tired,	then he is tireless.
When you are in a tizzy,	then he is together.
When you are toothless,	then he has teeth for you.
When you are tormented,	then he can soothe.

When you are touched,	then he is touching.
When you are touchy,	then he is tough.
When you are toxic,	then he is nontoxic.
When you are traitorous,	then so was Judas.
When you are trashy,	then he is treasured.
When you are tricky,	then he is never tricked.
When you are in trouble,	then he can be there on the double.
When you are a troublemaker,	then he is not troublesome.
When you are truant,	then he is never tardy.
When you are tuneless,	then he is tuneful.
When you are a twerp,	then he was no brat.
When you are a tyrant,	then he does not oppress.
When you are ugly,	then he is superficial.
When you are ulcerous,	then he can heal you.
When you are unable,	then he is able.
When you are unaccepted,	then he is acceptable.
When you are unappealing,	then he is appealing.
When you are unaccommodating,	then he is accommodating.
When you are unaccomplished,	then he is accomplished.
When you are unamused,	then he is amused.
When you are unappreciated,	then he is appreciated.
When you are unassertive,	then he is assertive.
When you are unaware,	then he is aware.
When you are unbalanced,	then he is well balanced.
When you are unbearable,	then he is unbeatable.
When you are unbecoming,	then he is becoming.
When you are an unbeliever,	then he is believable.
When you are unblessed,	then he gives blessings.
When you are uncanny,	then he is canny.
When you are uncertain,	then he is certain.

When you are uncivilized,	then he is civilized.
When you are unclean,	then he is clean.
When you are unclear,	then he is clear.
When you are uncomfortable,	then he is a comfort.
When you are uncommitted,	then he is committed.
When you are unconcerned,	then he is concerned.
When you are unconscious,	then he is conscious of you.
When you are uncontrollable,	then he is self-controlled.
When you are unconvinced,	then he is convincing.
When you are uncooperative,	then he is cooperative.
When you are undecided,	then he is decided.
When you are undependable,	then he is dependable.
When you are undercut,	then he is clean-cut.
When you are an underdog,	then he overcame.
When you are underhanded,	then he is over the counter.
When you are undermined,	then he is determined.
When you are underneath,	then he is above.
When you are undernourished,	then he has nourishment for you.
When you are underpaid,	then he can manage.
When you are underprivileged,	then he is privileged.
When you are undetermined,	then he is determined.
When you are undignified,	then he is dignified.
When you are undiplomatic,	then he is diplomatic.
When you are undirected,	then he directs.
When you are undisciplined,	then he is disciplined.
When you are undutiful,	then he is dutiful.
When you are uneasy,	then he can put you at ease.
When you are uneducated,	then he is educated.
When you are unemotional,	then he is emotional.
When you are unemployed,	then he can put you to work.

When you are unending,	then he is the living end.
When you are unenjoyable,	then he is enjoyable.
When you are unenlightened,	then he is enlightening.
When you are unenthusiastic,	then he is enthusiastic.
When you are unessential,	then he is essential.
When you are inexperienced,	then he is experienced.
When you are unfair,	then he is fair.
When you are unfaithful,	then he is faithful and true.
When you are unfeeling,	then he has feeling.
When you are unfitting,	then he is fitting.
When you are unforgiving,	then he is forgiving.
When you are unfortunate,	then he can make you fortunate.
When you are unfriendly,	then he is friendly.
When you are unfruitful,	then he is fruitful.
When you are ungainly,	then he is gainly.
When you are ungenerous,	then he is generous.
When you are ungentle,	then he is gentle.
When you are ungentlemanly,	then he is gentlemanly.
When you are unGodly,	then he is Godly.
When you are ungovernable,	then he governs.
When you are ungraceful,	then he is graceful.
When you are ungracious,	then he is gracious.
When you are ungrateful,	then he is grateful.
When you are ungratifying,	then he is gratifying.
When you are unguarded,	then he can have you guarded.
When you are unhallowed,	then he is hallowed.
When you are unhappy,	then he can make you happy.

When you are unhealthy,	then he can make you healthy.
When you are unheard,	then he is heard.
When you are unhelpful,	then he is helpful.
When you are unheroic,	then he is heroic.
When you are unholy,	then he is holy.
When you are unimaginative,	then he has imagination.
When you are unimportant,	then he is important.
When you are unimpressed,	then he is impressive.
When you are uninspired,	then he is inspirational.
When you are unindustrious,	then he is industrious.
When you are uninfluenced,	then he is influential.
When you are uninformed,	then he is informative.
When you are uninnovative,	then he is innovative.
When you are uninstructed,	then he is instructor.
When you are uninsured,	then he can insure you.
When you are unintellectual,	then he is intellectual.
When you are uninteresting,	then he is interesting.
When you are uninvigorating,	then he is invigorating.
When you are uninvolved,	then he is involved.
When you are unjust,	then he is just.
When you are unjustifiable,	then he is justified.
When you are unkind,	then he is kind.
When you are unknown,	then he is known.
When you are unlawful,	then he is lawful.
When you are unlearned,	then he is learned.
When you are unlighted,	then he is lighted.
When you are unliked,	then he likes.
When you are unlively,	then he is lively.
When you are unloved,	then he loves.
When you are unlucky,	then he can bless you.

When you are unmannerly,	then he has manners.
When you are unmeaning,	then he has meaning and purpose.
When you are unmentionable,	then he is mentionable.
When you are unmerciful,	then he is merciful.
When you are unmindful,	then he is mindful.
When you are unmotivated,	then he can motivate you.
When you are unmusical,	then he is musical.
When you are unnatural,	then he is natural.
When you are unnecessary,	then he is necessary.
When you are unneeded,	then he needs you.
When you are unobliging,	then he is obliging.
When you are unobservant,	then he is observant.
When you are unnoteworthy,	then he is noteworthy.
When you are unnoticed,	then he notices you.
When you are unorganized,	then he is organized.
When you are unoriginal,	then he is original.
When you are unpardoned,	then he can pardon you.
When you are unpeaceful,	then he is peaceful.
When you are unpersuasive,	then he is persuasive.
When you are unpitied,	then he pities you.
When you are unplanned,	then he may have plans for you.
When you are unpleasant,	then he is pleasant.
When you are unpleasing,	then he is pleasing.
When you are unpoetic,	then he is poetic.
When you are unpopular,	then he is popular.
When you are unpolished,	then he is polished.
When you are unpractical,	then he is practical.
When you are unpredictable,	then he is predictable.
When you are unprepared,	then he is prepared.

When you are unprincipled,   then he has principle.
When you are unproductive,   then he is productive.
When you are unprofessional,   then he is professional.
When you are unprofitable,   then he is profitable.
When you are unprogressive,   then he is progressive.
When you are unpromising,   then he is promising.
When you are unprosperous,   then he is prosperous.
When you are unprotected,   then he can protect you.
When you are unreachable,   then he can reach you.
When you are unready,   then he is ready.
When you are unreal,   then he is real.
When you are unrealistic,   then he is realistic.
When you are unreasonable,   then he is reasonable.
When you are unredeemed,   then he can redeem.
When you are unrefined,   then he is refined.
When you are unrefreshed,   then he is refreshing.
When you are unrelaxed,   then he can relax you.
When you are unreliable,   then he is reliable.
When you are unreligious,   then he is religion.
When you are unremembered,   then he remembers.
When you are unreserved,   then he is reserved.
When you are unrested,   then he can give you rest.
When you are unrespectful,   then he is respectful.
When you are unresponsive,   then he is responsible.
When you are unrevenged,   then vengeance is his.
When you are unrewarded,   then he will reward you.
When you are unruly,   then he rules.
When you are unsafe,   then he is safe.
When you are unsaintly,   then he is saintly.
When you are unsanctified,   then he is sanctified.
When you are unsanitary,   then he is sanitary.

When you are unsatisfactory,   then he is satisfactory.
When you are unsatisfied,   then he can satisfy.
When you are unscrupulous,   then he has scruples.
When you are unseemly,   then he is seemly.
When you are unsettled,   then he is unshakable.
When you are unsheltered,   then he has shelter for you
When you are unskilled,   then he is skilled.
When you are unsociable,   then he is sociable.
When you are unsophisticated,   then he is sophisticated.
When you are unsound,   then he is sound.
When you are unspeakable,   then he is well spoken of
When you are unsportsmanlike,   then consider his conduct.
When you are unsteady,   then he is steady.
When you are unsuccessful,   then he is a success.
When you are unsure,   then he is sure.
When you are unsympathetic,   then he is sympathetic.
When you are untactful,   then he is tactful.
When you are untalented,   then he is talented.
When you are unteachable,   then he is teacher.
When you are unthankful,   then he is thankful.
When you are unthoughtful,   then he is thoughtful.
When you are unthrifty,   then he is thrifty.
When you are untidy,   then he is tidy.
When you are untimely,   then he is on time.
When you are untrustworthy,   then he is trustworthy.
When you are untruthful,   then he is the truth.
When you are unvaluable,   then he is valuable.
When you are unwanted,   then he can love you.
When you are an unwed mother, then keep the baby.
When you are unwelcome,   then you are welcome.
When you are unwholesome,   then he is wholesome.

When you are unwilling,	then he is willing.
When you are unwise,	then he is wise.
When you are unworthy,	then he is worthy.
When you are upset,	then he can settle you down.
When you are upside down,	then he can put you right side up.
When you are used,	then he does not abuse.
When you are useless,	then he is useful.
When you are a vagabond,	then he is vivid.
When you are vain,	then he is valiant.
When you are valueless,	then he is valuable.
When you are a vandal,	then he is no scoundrel.
When you have VD or AIDS,	then you need the VIP.
When you are vengeful,	then vengeance is his.
When you are a vermin,	then he is victorious.
When you are vexed,	then he can undo the hex.
When you are vicious,	then he is no savage.
When you are a victim,	then he is vigilant.
When you are a vigilante,	then he is vigilant.
When you are a villain,	then he is not vile.
When you are vindictive,	then vengeance is his.
When you are violent,	then he is nonviolent.
When you are voiceless,	then he is heard.
When you are voodoo,	then he is taboo.
When you are vulgar,	then he is refined.
When you are vulnerable,	then he is no vulture.
When you are wacky,	then he is not tacky.
When you are wanton,	then he has restraint.
When you are warlike,	then he is peaceful.
When you are washed-up,	then he is not washed-out.

When you are wasteful,	then he is conservative.
When you are wayfarer,	then he can be home.
When you are weak,	then he is strong.
When you are weak-kneed,	then he has backbone.
When you are weak-minded,	then he is strong-minded.
When you are wearing,	then he is durable.
When you are wearisome,	then he is not wearing.
When you are weary,	then he can give you rest.
When you are a weasel,	then he is no snake.
When you are weird,	then he is not strange.
When you are not well-off,	then he is well-to-do.
When you are a wench,	then he is not wicked.
When you are a whore,	then "sin no more."
When you are wild,	then he can tame you.
When you are willful,	then he does God's will.
When you are a wino,	then he is sober.
When you are wishy,	then he is not washy.
When you are a witch,	then he is no wizard.
When you are witless,	then he is witty.
When you are woeful,	then he is wonderful.
When you are worldly,	then he is heavenly.
When you are a worm,	then he can make a butterfly of you.
When you are worrisome,	then he is not worried
When you are worthless,	then he is worthy.
When you are wounded,	then so was he.
When you are a wretch,	then he is not wretched.
When you are wrong,	then he is right for you.

The Lord Is Everything from A to Z

The Lord, he is the Alpha and Omega.
He is altogether, always, and ancient,
and he is age-old, allied, and ardent.

The Lord is alive and alert.
He is all right and admired,
and he is able and adept.

The Lord is aboveboard.
He is accurate and active,
and he is actual and adapt.

The Lord is absolute and advocator.
He is adorable and he is affable
and affectable and affirmable.

The Lord is amiable, amicable, and ample.
He is analytic, amusing, and appealing,
and appreciative and apprehensive.

The Lord is appropriate, articulate, and arbitrator.
He is assured, austere, and astounding,
and he is aware and awesome.

The Lord is beloved and belongs.
He is believed and blameless,
and he is brave and bright.

"The Lord is the bright and morning star,"
seated at the right hand of the power of God from afar,
and he knows exactly how you are and he cares exactly
     how you are.

The Lord he never boasts
but he is known coast to coast,
and he is filled with the Holy Ghost.

The Lord is balanced and balmy.
He is bang-up and benevolent,
and he is big and blessed.

The Lord is bold and bona fide.
He is brainy and brilliant
and he is brother.

The Lord is Christ and Christmas.
He is chummy, classy, and civil
and he is clean and clear.

The Lord is calm and collected.
He is competent and confident,
and he is careful and cautious.

The Lord is candid and candor.
He is catching and cautionary,
and he is certainly a celebrity.

The Lord is concerned and cares.
He is considerate and compassionate,
and he is both courageous and conqueror.

The Lord he is champion and charisma.
He is charming, chaste, and cherished,
and he is chief, chipper, and chivalrous.

The Lord is coherent and colorblind.
He is colossal, comforter, and commander,
and he is commendable, companion, and company.

The Lord is complete, complex, and compulsory.
He is comprehensible and comprehensive,
and he is conceivable and concise.

The Lord is conclusive and concrete.
He is conducive and conductor
and he is conscientious.

He is consistent, cool, and cooperative.
He is creator, curator, and counselor
and courteous, correct, and direct.

He is not dangerous nor derelict.
He knows his duty and he does it,
and he is dynamic and dynamite.

He is delightful and dedicated.
He is determined, dependable,
and he is deliberate and durable.

The Lord is dear and deserving.
He is disciplined and distinguished,
and he is devoted, devout, and demure.

He is Emmanuel the Emancipator.
He is Everlasting and Eternal.
He is Easter and Electric.

He is enchanting and entertaining.
He is enjoyable and essential
and equitable and energetic.

The Lord is earnest and eager.
He is efficient and effective
and elegant and eloquent.

The Lord is emotional and eminent.
He is empowered and enlightened,
and he is especially encouraging.

He is Faithful and true.
He is fruitful and rules.
He is not hateful or rude.

The Lord is free and is freedom.
He is free willed and free spoken,
and free handed and free hearted.

The Lord is friend, friendly, and folksy.
He is frisky, funny, and fundamental,
and he is fair, frank, and futuristic.

He is fabulous, fantastic, and fascinating.
He is famous, familiar, and favorable.
He is factual, formal, and fine.

The Lord is fine as unfermented wine.
He stands straight like a pine.
He has a divine mind.

He is part of the Godhead.
He is second to God
and he is Godly.

He is first-rate and God's # One Son.
He is forthright and forthcoming.
He is for ever and for ever more.

The Lord is forgiving and giving.
He is gracious and generous,
and he is grand and great.

He is generally gallant.
He is genuine, glorious,
he is gainly and gentle.

He has no bad habits.
He is gentle as a rabbit.
He keeps holy the Sabbath.

He is our hope and haven.
He is our heart and health.
He is our honor and hero.

"The Lord is Emmanuel" and immortal.
He is impressionable, incomparable,
he is intermediary and intercessor.

The Lord is ideal, idealized, and idealistic.
He is illuminating, influential, and implicit,
and immaculate, intimate, and impartial.

The Lord is incorruptible and informative.
He is indefaticable and imaginative
and invariable and imperative.

The Lord is impeccable and impressive.
He is independent and an individual
and he is ingenious and important.

The Lord is innocent and inspirational.
He is intelligent and interesting.
He is intent and invincible.

The Lord is joyful and jubilant.
He is jaunty and he was Jewish
and he is "jam up and jelly tight."

The Lord is the Key and he is keen.
He is knowledgeable and kindly,
and he is kinder than kind.

The Lord is logical and level-headed
and he is likable and lovable
and he is lowly and loyal.

He is laborious and law-abiding
and he is a leader and learned
and he is lasting and lauded.

The Lord is not lazy nor late.
He always keeps his date
and Jesus is our fate.

Jesus is the One for you.
He can give you life anew.
He is a miracle come true.

He is marvelous.
He is miraculous.
He is magnanimous.

He is moral.
He is magical.
He is mystical.

He is magic.
He is majestic.
He is monotheistic.

He is mature.
He is a martyr.
He is mediator.

He is mighty.
He is master.
He is masculine.

He is the most.
He is magnifico.
He is magnificent.

He is mately.
He is manager.
He is memorable.

He is mindful.
He is merciful.
He is meaningful.

He is not mean to me.
He is the Light by which we see.
He is meant to be ours and I hope you agree.

He is not worldly.
He is the world to me.
He is Heavenly you all see.

The Lord is manna from Heaven.
He is meek, modest, and honest.
He is near, nigh, nice, and noble.

The Lord is not nosy nor is he notorious.
He is neither nearsighted nor narrow-minded.
He is naturally natural, neat, and he is nonviolent.

The Lord is outgoing and open-hearted
and he is observant and objective.
He is orderly and organized.

He learned obedience
by the things he suffered.
He was obedient until death.

He is prudent and he was a student.
He is not prejudice nor preconceived.
He is prepped, prepared, and prescribed.

He is patient and perfect.
He is peaceful and pleasant.
He is persistent and priceless.

More powerful than money.
He is sweeter than honey.
He is sober and sunny.

With him, you will prosper.
He is precious and pleasing.
He does not believe in teasing.

He is the Prince of life.
He can handle the strife.
He can get you a good wife.

He is the Prince of peace.
His reign will never ever cease.
He can wash sins white as fleece.

He is paradise and precise.
He is profound and pure.
He is popular and quick.

The Lord is quaint and quiet.
He is quickened in the spirit.
He is reverent and rational.

He is remarkable and respectable.
He is reasonable and reputable.
He is responsible and reliable.

The Lord is real and real-life.
He is receptive and receptor
and resourceful and respectful.

He is ready and radiant.
He is reserved and resolved
and he is revered and renowned.

The Lord is rhythm and rhyme.
He is redemption and resurrection
and he is ransom, religion, and scripture.

He is sugar and spice
and everything nice,
once, twice, thrice.

The Lord is sane and stable,
and he is safe and secure.
He is sensitive and sinless.

He is the Lord our Super.
He is a Super Sport.
He is Sporty.

He is super normal.
He is a Super Star.
He is supernatural.

He is super.
He is superb.
He is superior.

He is sacred.
He is saintly.
He is a Savior.

He is salvation.
He is a shepherd.
He is sanctified.

He is sanitary.
He is scholarly.
He is scholastic.

He is sensible.
He is stringent.
He is sentimental.

He is sharp.
He is serene.
He is serious.

He is single for now.
He is single-hearted.
He is single-minded.

He is smart.
He is savant.
He is smooth.

He is soft.
He is sound.
He is social.

He is Special.
He is Someone
He is Soulful.

He is spiritual.
He is spirited.
He is spirit.

He is spontaneous.
He is sophisticated.
He is a square shooter.

He is staunch.
He is stand-up.
He is steadfast.

He is steady.
He is spunky.
He is splendor.

He is stern.
He is strict.
He is strategic.

He is successful.
He is supportive.
He is sufficient.

He is sure.
He is strong.
He is supreme.

He is sweet.
He is swell.
He is swift.

He is surprising.
He is significant.
He is sympathetic.

He is splendid.
He is splendent.
He is splendorous.

He is sincere.
He is austere.
He persevered.

He stood his ground,
and uttered not a sound,
until he was death bound.

We learned for what he stood.
He is strict for our own good.
He earned his priesthood.

"Salvation is free."
He is One of three.
He is the way to be.

He is strong like an oak.
He enjoys a true clean joke.
He will never poke fun at anyone.

He is not into himself.
He loves most everyone else.
To children Sí His lap is a shelf.

The Lord is specific and terrific.
He is scientific and therapeutic,
and stupendous and tremendous.

The Lord is tried and torrid.
He is tolerant and triumphant.
He is talented and treasured.

The Lord is tuneful and temperate.
He is traditional and transcendental.
He is thankworthy and trustworthy.

The Lord is tidy and thrift.
He is thrilling and touching.
He is together and totally.

He is top-notch and take-charge.
He is tenderhearted and true-life.
He is true hearted and true love.

He is true blue.
He does love you.
This is honestly true.

"He is the true way."
"He is the true vine."
"He is the true Light."

"He is the Truth of God."
"He is the Lamb of God."
"He is the Son of God."

He is teacher and tactful.
He is tasteful and thankful.
He is truthful and thoughtful.

He is tame and tough.
He is thorough and timely
and he is timely and up-to-date.

He is ultra and ultimate.
He is urgent and uplifting.
He is useful and unanimous.

He is unquestionable and unregulated.
He is unmistakable and unworldly
and unforgettable and universal.

He is understood.
He is understanding.
He is not underestimated.

The Lord is vigilant and valiant.
He is virtuous and victorious
and he is very valuable.

He is wise.
He is witty.
He is wishful.

He is wonderful.
He is wondrous.
He is a wonder.

He is whole.
He is wholesome
and he is wide-awake.

He is praiseworthy.
He is noteworthy.
He is worthy.

Have you heard the Word?
"The Word was with God
and the Word was God."

The Lord is the Word and the Way.
He is warmhearted and well mannered.
He is wakeful, watchful, and not wasteful.

Extra! Extra!
Read all about
Jesus the Christ.

He is extra nice.
He is extra special.
He is extra righteous.

He is extramundane.
He is extrasensory.
He is extraterrestrial.

He is extraordinary.
He is extremely smart.
He is exceptionally quick.

He is exact.
He is exalted.
He is excellent.

He is exhilarating.
He is exceptional.
He is our example.

He is exciting.
He is exclusive.
He is executive.

He is explanatory.
He is exclusive.
He is executor.

He is expert.
He is explicit.
He is experienced.

He is expositive.
He is expressive.
He is extensive.

He is exquisite.
He is exuberant.
He is expedient.

Yule does mean Christmas.
He is positive like yes.
Christ is zealous.

The Lord is Everything from A to Z.
He can make the blind to see.
He has told us how to be.

Amen

I Would Like to Be Like

I would like to be alert.
I would like to be brave.
I would like to be compassionate
I would like to be devout.
I would like to be earnest.
I would like to be faithful.
I would like to be grateful.
I would like to be honest.
I would like to be immaculate.
I would like to be joyful.
I would like to be kind.
I would like to be loving.
I would like to be merciful.
I would like to be nice.
I would like to be open-hearted.
I would like to be perfect.
I would like to be quaint.
I would like to be respectable.
I would like to be sincere.
I would like to be thoughtful.
I would like to be understanding.
I would like to be virtuous.
I would like to be warm-hearted.
I would like to be extra special.
I would like to be positive like yes.
I would like to be zealous.
I would like to be like
The Lord Jesus Christ.
Amen

I Don't Know Much but I Do Know This

I don't know much, but I do know this,
I have never seen eyes kinder than his,
and they filled my mind and heart with bliss.

The vision was in black and white
but it was still quite a sight,
on that special night.

He is very kind and this is true.
His eyes appeared from out of the blue.
I do honestly hope to be with God and Jesus, too.

He was good with me, my friend.
He was good for me, my friend.
He was good to me, my friend.

He was life and he is life.
He can end your troubles and strife
and he can solve any problems in your life.

He told us how to live our life.
He showed us how to live our life.
He gave his life so we could have life.

It was out of love and obedience that he died,
and I honestly know he was crucified,
and I honestly have not lied.

Then he was raised from the dead
and it was just as Jesus had said.
For him there was no deathbed.

He died for us and he lives for us.
In him, you must obey and trust
and you must try, you must.

Try for God.
Try for Jesus.
Try for yourself.

Amen

A Reason to Live and a Heart to Give

I was pitiful you see.
But don't you pity me.
He showed pity on me
and he had mercy on me.

I am getting better day by day.
Jesus has shown me the way
to be and to behave.
Not only did he save

my wretched lost soul
but he made me whole.
Now this I do tell,
he made me well.

He took away my sin;
for I was sin sick then.
He took away my pain
and he made me sane.

He took away the rot
and he helped me a lot.
He took away my trouble
and he restored my bubble.

He taught me to mind
and to always be kind.
He taught me to obey
what they have to say.

He taught me to lean on him.
Now I throw my cares to him.
He taught me how to live
and he taught me to give.

He let me live
and he did give
me a reason to live
and a heart to give.

I do give to him my heart.
It is a good place to start.
My heart goes out to God and Holy, too.
And I do hope that they are not blue.

Amen

Thy Number One Son, Thy Will Be Done

We need Christ Jesus.
We need you within us.

We need Satan to stop.
We need it an awful lot.

We need to get it together.
We need a life much better.

We need better weather.
I do need to sleep better.

I need to quit smoking
and I am not joking

I need a helpmate.
I need a soul mate.

I need to die and go to heaven,
so that I can be with you seven.

Jesus hear this prayer.
Jesus please be aware.

We ask these things, oh, # One Son
but we all do know, thy will be done.

We need you, our Friend.
We need you to the end.

Amen

Sweet Jesus, Please Please Us

Sweet Jesus, please please us.
Please make us well
so we can tell

how you pulled us through
our dark days and our blues.
Sweet Jesus, we do need you

to help us now and always.
We need you in all ways
and in a special way.

"Jesus, meek and mild,"
look upon this sinful child.
Please help us not to be wild.

"Stick with us through thick and thin."
Please give us life anew again
and help us not to sin.

Be with us through good times and bad,
though we be happy or very sad.
Please, Jesus, make us glad.

We love you, Jesus.
We need you, Jesus.
We have you, Jesus.

It's good of you
to love us, too,
and love you do.

Just your name
makes me sane
in my little brain.

Jesus, the sweetest name I know.
Sweet Jesus, please help us so
we can go in the way to go.

Amen

Please Stay and Get Away

Jesus, please stay,
teach us the way.

Teach us in thy way,
so we will not stray.

Teach us how to be,
so we can see thee.

Teach us to mind,
so you will be kind.

Please give us peace,
put our mind at ease.

Please keep us sane,
take away our pains.

Please take away our fears.
Please take away our tears.

Please take away our sadness.
Please fill us up with gladness.

Please take away our strife,
so we can live a good life.

Please take away our stress,
so we can do our very best.

Please keep us from Satan.
Enough already he has taken.

Enough already from us you took.
We are tired of your gobble de gook.

Get thee behind us, Satan.
Get away from us, Satan.

Jesus, please be near,
so that we will not fear.

Please watch over us.
Will you, sweet Jesus?

Please take care of us.
We do need you, Jesus.

Amen

We Do Need You

I have something to say
and I'm sure you'll agree.
It concerns the way
that we all should be.

I now do know ye,
and you know me,
There is something that is wrong, see.
There is something not right, you see.

We are a captive of sin
and we are a slave of sin.
We need to be born again
and to be set free from sin.

We need to be born of the spirit
and to be filled with the Holy Spirit.
We need you,
all of us do.

Every single one of us
do need you, Jesus.
We all need you within
so that we will not sin.

Do be
in me.
We all do need, Jesus,
we need you within us.

We do need to belong to you
so we will be strong with you.
We need you in our heart
that's a good place to start.

We need you in our mind
so we will always be kind.
We need you in our heart and mind
so we will always be smart and kind.

So please, Jesus, break the shackles that do bind,
please set us free from sin in our heart and mind.
Yes, we do need you all the most,
the Father, Son, and Holy Ghost.

Yes, we do need you and love you all.
There is absolutely none above you all.
Yes, to us, you are above all,
we do need and love you all.

Amen

I Am That I Am

Who is Honestly Honest?
Who is Certainly Certain?
Who is Perfectly Perfect?
Who is Especially Special?
Who is Altogether Together?

Our God is All and He is.
And God is The God I AM.
Jehovah is The God I AM.
Yahweh is The God I AM.
Javeh is The God I AM.

The Lord God is All.
He is Adonai-The Lord.
He is The Lord-The Master.
He is Elyon-The Most High.
He is God-The Supreme Being.

He is Almighty God.
He is Abba-The Father.
He is El-The Strong One.
He is Elohim-The Divine One.
He is El-Shaddai-The Mighty One.

God is over all,
and after all, he is above all,
and all in all, he is All.
He is All Powerful and All Knowing,
and although he knows of evil,

God is All Good.
All Good from A to Z,
and he sent his # One Son
to show us how to be you see,
to be all loving, caring, and obedient.

Our God is a Loving God.
Yes, God Himself is Love.
This is the way He is,
the way God is,
always.

God is All.
God The Father,
and his Son Jesus,
and the Holy Spirit,
they love you all always.

Amen

No One You See Is Greater Than He

Who makes the Sun come up and go down
and who makes the world go round and round?

Who makes the deaf to hear and the lame to walk
and who makes the blind to see and the dumb to talk?

Who cares for you and loves you, too
and who can make you feel brand-new?

Who can bring out the best in you
and who can cure you of the blues?

Who is as Good as Good can be
and who is the Best of the Best?

Who is good to us, who can pardon us,
and who let his Son suffer and die for us?

Who is responsible for saving our lost souls
and who is responsible for making us whole?

Who is all knowing and Almighty?
No one you see is greater than he.

God is good, better, best.
He is better than the rest

of creation for sure,
a sensation for sure.

Amen

God Is Great. God Is Good. God Is Love.

Please tell me
what did thee see
when thee looked in me?

Was it my tormented heart,
which was nearly torn apart
from an extremely early start?

Was it my tormented mind,
which Satan and sin did bind,
that caused thee to be so kind?

Why are thee oh so kind?
Why did thee heal my heart and mind?
Why did thee break all of the shackles that did bind?

Why did thee heal me?
Why did thee help me?
Why did thee love me?

Why did thee feel for me?
Why did thee care for me?
Why did thee live for me?

Thee made me live.
Thee made me give.
Thee made me love.

Thee made me cry.
Thee made me try.
Thee made me why?

Thee saved me from sin.
Thee are my Best Friend.
Thee made me able to win.

Without you, I am nowhere.
With you, I am somewhere.
Yes, you made me aware.

Without you, I am no one.
With you, I am someone.
You made me love you.

"God is Great."
"God is Good."
"God is Love."

Amen

I Do Love You

I wonder when I will finish this book.
I cannot believe all the time it took.

and while we are on the subject,
I will not quit until it is perfect.

I have worked on it for a few years.
I know I caused Jesus a few tears.

I did curse when I could not get it right.
I did curse morning, noon, and at night.

But he was patient with me and let me live.
I did live because Jesus the Christ did give.

I did walk away from it many a time
but I did always come back to rhyme.

I do wonder why I was such a big nut
and why I did give it to such a big nut.

I gave it to Satan because I did not care.
And now of this I am sure and well aware.

I wish that I had not given it to that Satan.
Because years to straighten it has taken.

Yes, I do wonder about a lot of things,
like Satan trying to drive us all insane.

It is a wonder that I am not insane crazy.
Satan, he tried to make my memory hazy.

What in the world has gotten into you
and how come you do us like you do?

I now know how come you do us like you do,
you do know that time is running out for you.

Oftentimes, you did give us bad dreams
but we have learned you are a bad dream.

Every so often, you do raise your evil head
to try and make us all wish we were dead.

You would kill us if Jesus would let you
but he holds the key to death and not you.

You did mess up my life or so it seems.
You nearly kept me off the dream team.

I wonder what goes on at sport events,
with Satan making deals in wet cement.

You simply cannot tell about any of it
because Satan takes the fun out of it.

Satan does give to some players power,
so that they will be the men of the hour.

They may think that they have taken Satan
but in reality it is they that have been taken.

"The world is not as it appears."
Making deals will lead to tears.

Please don't you make a deal for anything,
no food, money, sex, car, or diamond ring.

You can sell your soul for what you want
but make it to heaven for ever you won't.

But enough about you and more about him.
I am talking about the Great God Elohim.

I wonder how you came to be.
It is a mystery to me you see.

I wonder why you are the way you are.
I wonder how you made the many stars.

I wonder why you made this worthless skin,
which does lead us to all sorts of sexual sin.

I wonder if your having made Satan you do regret.
I bet you do regret having made him at all I do bet.

I know you do not regret having made this old earth,
However, we do look forward to it's brand-new birth.

I wonder when "wormwood" will hit this world,
which will destroy a third of this here old world.

With Satan, sin, and evildoers around this here world,
it is no wonder people go around hating this cold world.

I wonder how much longer this world will go round,
with fewer and fewer righteous people to be found.

I wonder why we do not all do what is right.
I wonder why we choose darkness to light.

I wonder what is beyond outer darkness.
One day I may get to ask his Highness.

I am glad he did rescue me from darkness.
I am glad we were all made in his likeness.

I wonder what you do look like.
You gave man and woman life.

Your creative imagination does amaze me,
from all the creatures to the deep blue sea.

You did create the day and the night.
I wonder what is behind your might.

You did tell us to live life right
and you did tell us not to fight.

I do not know how Jesus took it.
I could not have stood it one bit.

He was obedient unto death,
so that we all might have life.

I use to wonder what life was about
but now I do know without a doubt,

that life is a learning process for you and me,
so that we can all learn exactly how to be.

We are beaten in childhood to learn right from wrong,
so that eventually to Jesus the Christ, we will belong.

It is through all our suffering that we all do grow
and through all our experiences that we do know.

It is Jesus Christ you live for and not doctor death.
All should be concerned with life rather than death.

Life can be full of tests for you and me,
up until our very last breath you see.

I wonder about lots of things,
like will I see another spring.

I wonder when I will take my very last breath,
so give me liberty and give me life after death.

I do wonder who will take my miserable life,
for my faith and my belief in Jesus Christ.

I do wonder who my killer will be.
I do not know but I do forgive ye.

Oh, how can I hold it against thee?
when all ye did was end my misery.

May Jesus have mercy on thee.
All you did was to make me free.

I hope my killer
pulls the trigger

and sends me to
the three of you.

Will I die at the hand of man?
Will I die according to a plan?

It just could be Satan
when my life is taken.

It just could be that beast,
who sends me to the feast.

My killer just may be me.
It could very well be me.

I cannot forget my past.
I wonder if I shall last.

I remember it less than I use to.
Nothing but peace of mind will do.

A memory can be bad or good.
Think of the good, you should.

Forget the bad and remember the good.
Try and think the way that you should.

I wonder when I will be shot dead in the head.
Yes, I do wonder when my blood will run red.

I wonder will I have a sudden "second death"
after I have taken my last miraculous breath.

I wonder why miracle babies do die,
without being given a chance to try.

I wonder about the miracle of life.
I wonder why I haven't a good wife.

I wonder how your miracles work.
I do wonder why I was such a jerk.

I do wonder why I do like I do.
I wonder why you love me, too.

I wonder why you do like you do.
I do know that I do love you, too.

I might not understand you but this I do know,
that you and yours are running this here show.

I know that you and your Son do rule from above
and that you are Great, Good, and you are Love.

Amen

Love From Above

If I had my way,
we all would live in peace and harmony,
and all would always be as sweet as honey,
and no one would worry about love or money,
and all would always be sober, sunny, and funny,
and no one would absolutely never ever be angry.

If I had my way,
We all would know not hunger nor hard times,
and everyone would keep themselves in line,
and no one would ever need worry about time,
and everyone would be tender, loving, and kind,
and I would write and rhyme in my spare time.

If I had my way,
we all would know how to read and write.
we would live a life free from fright
and we all would live in the light.
We would never live by night
and we all would live right.

If I had my way,
there would be no sickness nor sin
and the world would be a safe and sane
place for children to live and to play in.
Yes, there would be sincerely no more sin
and all would be born anew and born again.

If I had my way,
there would be no suffering or pain or shame,
and all would be forgiven and with no blame,
and all would be as gentle as a lamb and tame,
and all would be able to hear, talk, and walk,
and there would be no deaf, dumb, or lame.

If I had my way,
there would be no crying, lying, or lust.
All would have heavenly bodies, not dust,
and everyone would make it and not bust.
All would be healthy and wealthy, they must,
and all in God and Jesus Christ† would trust.

If I had my way,
there would be no fussing, fighting, or strife,
and no one would use a gun, club, or knife,
and we would all have a wonderful life,
and we would be one and a good wife.

If I had my way,
I would have a good wife
and be able to handle strife.
I would have a good life
and be as sharp as a knife.

If I had my way,
I would have to be young again
and I would know what I know now then.
I would have a life free from sin
and I would depend on Jesus, my Friend.

If I had my way,
I would have me a home in Hawaii
and friendly folks would ask how are ye.
I would have me a car the color of my eyes
and mostly blue would be the color of the skies.

If I had my way,
folks would live on easy street
and folks would have solar heat,
for all folks to warm their seat,
and that and they would be neat.

If I had my way,
the weather would be nice and not hot or chilled,
and there would be no pollution from mills,
and the ground for food would be tilled,
and everyone would be spirit filled.

If I had my way,
everyone would share freely and no one would horde.
No one would be lonely, brokenhearted, or bored
as our spirits were lifted high and as we soared.
From our spirits we would serve the Lord.

If I had my way,
no one would be mean, cruel, or rough.
Of this everyone has had enough.
And as for the acting tough,
Jesus, you will not bluff.

If I had my way,
no one would be had, hurt, or harmed.
There would be no cause for alarm,
because hearts would be warm
and we would have charm.

If I had my way,
no one would smoke or take dope
but everyone with stress would cope.
And there would be no drunks or skunks
but everyone would have hope and spunk.

If I had my way,
no one would push, press, or shove.
Everyone would be as free as a dove.
There would be no hate but only love,
the kind of love that we have dreamed of.

If I had my way,
no one would have need for anything;
for all our needs would be met.
All we would need is love.
God's love from above.

If I had my way,
no one would ever kill
but all would will God's will.
So "Know that God is God and be still,"
and know that God is for me and you all for real.

If I had my way,
I would change a lot
but as you know, I do not.
So look to our God who is hot
and know that he gives it all he's got.

May God have his way.
God is Grand.
God is Great.
God is Good.
God is Love.

Amen

Love

Love is a very positive feeling.
Love is a warm feeling from within.
Love is a feeling like you never felt before.

Love makes you feel nice and neat.
Love makes you feel well and good.
Love makes you feel safe and sane.

Love makes a house a home.
Love is a warm heart, not a heart of stone.
Love is a safe and secure home, from which one
    does not roam.

Love is fine and dandy.
Love is sweeter than candy.
Love is being free and handy.

Love is being free from sin and worry.
Love is never having to say you are sorry.
Love is someone understanding in times of sorrow.

Love is a wonderful thing.
Love is better than gold or a diamond ring.
Love is splendor and better than just about most
    everything.

"Love is as strong as hate."
"Love the good and hate the evil."
"Love not sleep" and "Love not evil."

Love not money.
Love not funny.
Love not yummy.

"Love not the world."
Love it not boys and girls
or get caught up in its whirl.

Love not the strife.
Love not your life.
Do love your wife

Love your mother.
Love your brother.
Love one another.

Love is good.
Love as you should.
Love all the brotherhood.

Love is great.
Love we will always take.
Love one another for heaven's sake.

Love is grand.
Love is making a stand.
Love is the salvation of mankind.

Love is kind.
Love is kinder than kind.
Love is the kind of love from above.

Love is from above.
Love is gentle like a dove.
Love is nothing to be ashamed of.

Love is a heart full of mirth.
Love is the celebration of a new birth.
Love is "good will toward men and peace on earth."

Love was a salvation plan.
Love was nail-scarred hands.
Love was the redemption of man.

Love was a rib from Adam's side.
Love is man and woman side by side.
Love is forgiveness and putting sins aside.

Love is putting yourself behind you.
Love is putting the world behind you.
Love is putting Satan and sin behind you.

Love is to be set free from sin.
Love is bigger than Big Ben.
Love is when a loser wins.

Love is free and it we need.
Love is pure and it is sure.
Love is strong and lasts long.

Love is strong as steel.
Love is very calm and still.
Love is obedience to God's will.

Love is blind faith.
Love is patiently waiting.
Love is within heaven's gates.

Love is from the heart.
Love is from heaven.
Love is from God.

Love is concerned, considerate, and compassionate.
Love is worship, fellowship, and friendship.
Love is caring, sharing, and giving.

Love is amazing grace and mercy.
Love is having a saved soul.
Love is being whole.

Love is being helped.
Love is helping others.
Love is helping yourself.

Love is living a Godly life.
Love is dying a Christian death.
Love is eternity with God and Christ.

"Love thy enemy."
"Love thy brother."
"Love thy neighbor."

Love Father.
Love Jesus.
Love Holy.

Love from above,
we can't get enough of.
God is Good, Great, and Love.

Amen

All You Need Is Love

If your heart is broken
and you are left wide open.
All you Need is Love.

When you are nearly insane
and feel the strain in your brain.
All you Need is Love.

If you are really sad
and you are not at all glad.
All you Need is Love.

When you are very lonely
and no one has eyes for you only.
All you Need is Love.

If you are down and—out
and don't know what life is all about.
All you Need is Love.

When you have been used
and you have been abused.
All you Need is Love.

If you have given up hope
and are at the end of your rope.
All you Need is Love.

When you are no longer strong
and you can stand no more,
then "stand still and know"

"God is God."
"God is Love."
"God is Good."

"God is Great."
God is God
and there is none other.

Jesus is Jesus
and he is our Big Brother.
Jesus is Great.

God is Greatest.
Jesus is Great for all.
God is Greatest of all.

Amen

The Right Diet

Food for Thought

Recipe:
Go to Jesus, who loves you,
to get to God, who loves you, too.
Seek God by studying his Word The Bible,
and be like his Word, the sweet Lord Jesus Christ.
Seek God's face by living and doing right,
and being righteous, and he will be in sight.

Results:
The closer you get to God,
the more weight you will lose.
The closer you get to God,
the more tears you will cry.
The closer you get to God,
the more you will know why
God loves you, "God is Love."
Warning: Please be aware of this diet.
You could dehydrate
if you became aware
of all the love God has for you all at once.
Amen

The Righteous Road?

The so-called righteous road
is actually a narrow pathway.
So if you carry a heavy load
or if you have a heavy burden,
then lighten the burden of life
and be enlightened by Christ.
Then cast all your cares on him;
for he really does care for you.
It is something you all can do
and Christ will help you all, too.
He can give you a brand-new start
and get you the desires of your heart.
So walk the straight and narrow
and travel it straight like an arrow.
Amen

Will I Make It?

Will I make it to heaven or not?
I do not know but I hope a lot.
Heaven or hell,
which shall it be?

I cannot tell,
which it shall be.
I do not know how
but I will make it somehow.

To be with the seven
I will have to make it to heaven
and see them for real.
They know how I feel

about them and all.
We will have a ball.
It may be a while
before we can smile,

Suffering suckatash,
we will have a bash.
I have been as bad as bad can be you see.
I hope God kept me innocent of blasphemy.

Do not blaspheme the Holy Spirit.
Don't even come close or near it.
"It is the only unforgivable sin."
Do it and you simply will not win.

Be a winner with Jesus Christ,
and grab ahold of eternal life.
Hope and pray for the best,
so you will have eternal rest

with The Father, the Son, and The Holy Ghost;
for they are the Ones who do love us the most.

Amen

I Hope I Do and You Do Too

Will I ever make it to paradise,
way up high above the blue skies?

Will I ever make it to paradise?
Maybe so, as sure as a bird flies.

Will I ever make it to paradise
and again get to see God's eyes?

Will I ever make it to paradise?
If I do, it will be a big surprise.

Will I ever make it to paradise?
I do hope to and win the prize.

Will I ever make it to paradise?
I hope I do and you do likewise.

If I am ever to make it to paradise,
I must do right and for ever be wise.

Amen

We're Gonna Make It with Some Help From Our Friend

We're gonna make it with some help from our Friend.
We're gonna make it and not fake it.
We're gonna give it our all and do it.

We're gonna make it with some help from our Friend.
We're gonna try and not cry.
We're gonna try and not lie.

We're gonna make it with some help from our Friend.
We're not gonna use or abuse people.
We're not gonna harm or alarm people.

We're gonna make it with some help from our Friend.
We're gonna put the past behind us.
We're gonna look forward to Jesus.

We're gonna make it with some help from our Friend.
We're gonna mind ye and be kind.
We're gonna know all and all grow.

We're gonna make it with some help from our Friend.
We're "the salt of the earth."
We're going for a new birth.

We're gonna make it with some help from our Friend.
We're not gonna wait until time is at an end.
We're gonna overcome the world, Satan, and sin.

We're gonna make it with some help from our Friend.
We're not gonna lose but we're gonna win.
We're gonna choose righteousness over sin.

We're gonna make it with some help from our Friend.
We're gonna love ye until the end and then our Friend.
We're gonna worship you and yours for ever our Friend

We're gonna make it with some help from our Friend.
From the One who helped save our soul and save us
    from sin.
From Jesus Christ our Lord and Saviour who did take
    us in.

We're gonna make it with some help from our Friend.
From the One who is our Good Friend,
who has helped us time and time again.

We're gonna make it with some help from our Friend.
From the One who paid the price for our sins
and we need you, Sweet Jesus Christ. Amen.

We're Gonna Do It Christ's Way or No Way at All

Well, lift your head, raise your hands, shout, and sing.
I'm gonna tell ya about the good news the King came
    to bring.
The good news it went out with a ring and to it you
    should for ever cling.

"God is Good, God is Great."
"God is Love, God is not hate."
"God is Grand, God is First-Rate."

The Father, Son, and Holy Ghost in One
and they love us each and every one.
I tell you it's time to get right, hon.

No time to play, so don't delay.
The time is near and it is nearly here.
So get ready for God and Jesus the Christ.

So do it for God and do it for Christ.
You have to try hard, you have to do right.
You must obey God's Word, try with all your might.

They didn't take but did give.
Don't you take but you give,
and just you live and let live.

Don't smoke, no joke.
Don't chew, it will not do.
"Be of sober mind," be kind.

We're nearing the end so don't bend.
Not much longer can it take so don't break.
The time is nearly upon us so don't fuss or cuss.

The time is now and you know how.
So do go for neo and go for now.
"For him, every knee shall bow."

It's time to prepare, it's getting late.
So get right, get ready, and don't hesitate.
He is our fate, so don't wait and get straight.

Time is running out
without any doubt.
Listen for a shout.

Time is slipping away.
Tomorrow is a new day.
Get ready and don't delay.

Are you ready
with confetti?
Hold steady.

Steady as she goes.
Everybody knows
when he shows.

He can heal your body, mind, and soul.
He loves the children, middle-aged, and old,
and just exactly how to be, we all have been told.

So get renewed, get ready, and get right with God.
So tune in, turn on, and get down with Christ.
So put off the old you and put on the new.

Christians, there's a new day coming.
Christians, Jesus will soon be coming.
Christians, it'll be his second coming.

Get ready to meet Jesus in the air.
Get control of your life and of Satan beware.
Get rid of the sin in your life and get it out of there.

We'll proceed with speed,
make haste and don't waste,
because it's time to begin again.

Do now and begin.
Do be born again.
Do away with sin.

You can win over sin, time and time again.
You can do it today, so pray and don't stray.
You can do it tonight, so do right and don't fight.

With all intent,
don't relent.
Do repent.

No more sin for us at all.
No more hell for us at all.
No more mess for us at all.

We're gonna do it Christ's way or no way at all.
Amen

The Way I Am

I am the way I am
and you are the way you are.
I do things my way
and you do things your way.

I cannot change the way I am
and you cannot change the way you are.
But I a.m. can change the way I am
and I a.*m.* can change the way we are.

If you are way down
and you are hung up,
he can settle you down
and then lift you way up.

So get going in the right lane
and stay off the right of way.
"The church made herself ready."
You do hold fast and stay steady.

The past is water over the dam.
The future is don't be damned.
Please change our way.
God please do it today.

Please don't put us off or delay.
God please help us not to stray.
Please help us not to sin,
right up until the very end.

Amen

The Way of Life

Is my life like your life?
I hope not.
Is sin to be the way of life?
I hope not.
Is there no hope in your life?
I hope not.
Is Jesus absent from your life?
I hope not.
Is God Almighty sick or dead?
I hope not
Is America in for her downfall?
I hope not.
Is the world in for her dark age?
I hope not.
Amen.

The Perfect Female

She gets an early start
and is very warm at heart.
She is extremely wittily smart
and is not necessarily a work of art.

She may be pretty.
She may be not so pretty.
She may be ugly.
She may be not so ugly.

She is of civil tongue
and does not play dumb.
She may have a green thumb
and she does not have loud lungs.

She does not fuss and does not cuss
and she does in Jesus Christ trust.
She may or may not have a big bust
and she is totally into love, not lust.

Against sexual advances she does protest.
Perverted sex she does detest,
such as molesting, incest,
and all the rest.

Little children she astounds.
She does not fool around.
She is morally sound.
She never hounds.

She is no fool.
She obeys the rules.
She may be short or tall
and she may be big or small.

She is not into herself
and she loves everyone else.
She always tries to give it her all
and she loves everyone big or small.

She is young or old
and is both brave and bold.
She does as her husband has told
and "she does not wear jewelry or gold."

She may wear feminine lace
and does not paint her face.
She does at times make haste
and she is forgiven by grace.

She is gracious and giving
and she truly enjoys living.
She finds peace of mind at times
and she may find life hell at times.

She is in no way hell
and does what she does well.
Her soul she simply will not sell
and she always does as The Bible tells.

The Bible is her holy guidance
and she may suffer in silence.
She may have a driver's license
and she really abhors violence.

She does not fight
and does what is right.
She tries with all her might
and lives by day and not by night.

She is tough but not rough
and she does not dish it out.
She knows when enough is enough
and she knows what life is all about.

She can take stress.
You she will impress.
She is of modest dress
and her life is no mess.

Her life may be good or bad
and she may be happy or sad.
She may sometimes be glad
and she may sometimes be mad.

She is not a cheat
and may be petite.
She is real sweet
and she is real neat.

She is for real
& has a great zeal
for loving and living life,
and she does make a great wife.

She can put one in their place
and she knows her place.
She is not two faced
but she is an ace.

She is not rich
and is no witch.
She may be poor
but she is no bore.

She has all she ever needs
and she is not into greed.
Of her you should take heed
and she is a special breed.

She does not ever want
and she does not taunt.
She does not ever tease
and you she may please.

She does not ever waste
and she has good taste.
She can keep up the pace
and she never loses face.

She does not ever gamble
and she does not ramble.
She is a high moral example
and her character is ample.

She does not ever go on a fling
and she has anger that can sting.
She is not into clothes and things
and does not own a diamond ring.

She is not into stuff
and she knows her stuff.
She is not a put on or cut up
and she knows what is going down.

She knows good times.
She knows of bad times.
She does walk the line
and lets her light shine.

She knows of loneliness
and she knows of emptiness.
She does know of sadness
and she knows of happiness.

She does know of health and sickness
and she can be either healthy or sickly.
She knows of wealth and wickedness
and she is neither wealthy nor wicked.

She is neither lazy nor crazy
and she does not dilly or dally.
She is neither good nor bad
and she may have been had.

She may not be perfect yet
but she will be.
She will be you can bet,
just wait and see.

She may be weak
but he is strong.
She is no freak,
for him she longs.

"She loves to tell the story
of Jesus and all his glory."
She belongs to him you see
and she loves him honestly.

She always tells the truth
and may have a sweet tooth.
She is not as loose as a goose
and she is the queen of the roost.

She is quiet
and is not a riot.
She has something to say
and she can make your day.

She is of few words
and is not for the birds.
She has little to say
but can tell you the way.

She can tell you the one way to be,
out of the two ways to be you see.
She can tell you right from wrong,
so you will grow up to be strong.

She can change you alright,
so you will not live the night-life.
She can be a big influence in your life
and she can be a big affluence in your life.

She can mold your heart and mind,
so you will be smart and be kind.
She can mold your soul and spirit,
so you will be whole and with it.

Your problems she can help you to solve
and she can shower you with love.
She is quite a person you see,
she can help you to see.

She can be serious.
She is not injurious.
At sin she is furious
and she is not curious.

She can be funny
and is sweet as honey.
She is thrifty with money
and is nearly always sunny.

She can sing a song
and is never ever wrong.
By a higher power she is strong
and she can make you feel you belong.

She can give you real hope
and make you able to cope.
She does not toke or smoke

and she does not take dope.
She has nothing at all to drink.
She is not into money or mink,
and is sometimes in the pink,
and for herself she can think.

She thinks of others
and has very many brothers.
She treats you as she would another
and she is kind, considerate, and no bother.

She is proficient and efficient
and is patient and not impatient.
She is persistent and consistent
and is prudent and is a student.

She is adorable and loveable
and is reasonable and dependable
She is capable and honorable
and is reliable and is responsible.

She is especially special
and is honestly honest.
She is assuredly sure
and certainly certain,

of where she stands,
and of all the demands,
of the Lamb who commands,
who did die for man and woman.

She is not a worldly woman,
but she is a very Godly person
and a mother or sister to Christ.
The Perfect Female is a Christian.

Amen

The Perfect Mate

I have seen the man in the moon.
I think it is a picture of Adam.
I have seen the woman in the moon.
I think it is a picture of Eve.

He was the most subtle.
He started the trouble.
He did tempt Eve.
She did Adam.

It was the start of sin for man.
It started the downfall of man.
Now he has no legs.
They broke the eggs.

She did not give, but she did take.
Her own deathbed she did make.
One said, "Let them eat cake;"
for which death was her fate.

She did nag Samson to his near death
and his sanity was put to the test.
She did nag Samson with every breath
and of Samson, she got the best.

Her husband's sure death
did put David to the test.
David's lust for a female
was his temporary downfall.

She was my downfall
but it was my fault, too.
She did lust after me.
I did lust after her, too.

"The larger the bust,
the lower was my IQ"
I did say yes to lust,
to lust I did say I do.

I am damned if I do
and damned if I don't.
The females I do desire don't desire me.
The females I don't desire do desire me.

Some females are healthy
but they can be hell on ye.
Be careful.
Be prayful.

I'm a sucker for beauty,
I really do love a cutey.
My gal was a beauty.
She drove me kooky

I was blinded by her beauty for a while
but now I do see she was only a child.
She was just a child.
I was young and wild.

One would think that I had learned my lesson,
but good-looking women do still affect me now.
However, now I look upon women as a blessing
and there is only one woman for me now and how.

One on one is the way for you and me you see,
that is the way God intended for it to be you see.
Wait until you find the one who is right for you,
the one who is like you and thinks like you do.

One can find the right one for him or her,
if one spends a little time with him or her.
Get to know and understand one another well
and you all will not live a life that is a pure hell.

"One can go a lot further if you do not go all the way."
Why ruin a good friendship, when friends you can stay.
It is just not worth all the pleasure and the pain you see.
If you go to bed together, it is a loss and no gain you see.

One can have other problems than a mate.
Life is full of pitfalls that just will not wait.
There is Satan, sin, men, and dogs that
can treat you like you are a big dirty rat.

One knows there is something that can be said
about killers, thieves, whores, and crackheads.
There is ample of hope, even if you are on dope.
But you must come clean, you know what I mean.

One should hope and pray; for there is a better way.
Try the straight and narrow way and don't stray.
Don't think that you are the one and only one.
because the world is just full of people hon.

He may think he is the only one.
She may think she is number one.
He may think there is only himself.
She may think there is no one else.

He may think he is something else,
but he is not much at all.
She may think she is something else,
but she is not much at all.

He may think he is a super sport
but all he is, is really a bad tort.
She may think she is a sex goddess
but all she is, is really immodest.

He may think he is going out
in a glorious big blaze of glory.
Neither knows what life is about,
for her it may be the same story.

"The glory of young men is their strength:
and the beauty of old men is the gray head."
"For a man indeed ought not to cover his head,
For as much as he is the image and glory of God."

"But the woman is the glory of man.
For the man is not of the woman;
but the woman of the man.
Man was not created for the woman; but woman for man."

"God created Adam and Eve
and not Adam and Steve."
On Jesus you must believe,
so glory you will receive.

"You will receive a new name,"
If in you all do make it to glory.
"A man's long hair is his shame."
"A woman's long hair is her glory."

"A woman should not ever braid her hair,"
but she should keep clean and take care,
Treat people fair and you will get there.
No matter what they call you, be square.

A "woman is the weaker sex,"
but I think she is the sweeter sex.
Man is more violent of the two,
but violence just simply will not do.

He can be in love with money
or your heart he can break.
She can be as sweet as honey
or be as mean as a snake.

He can be extremely handsome
but he can be ugly and then some.
She can be nice to look upon outside
but she can be ugly within the inside.

It is good to imagine life with them.
It is hard to imagine life without them.
Sometimes it is hard to live with them.
Sometimes it is hard to live without them.

Sometimes he may die but so may she.
Sometimes he may lie but so may she.
Sometimes he may try but so may she.
Sometimes he may cry but so may she.

Sometimes they don't get along
but they were made for each other.
He has tried to conquer the world.
They have tried to conquer each other.

They are partly responsible for the downfall of man.
They are partly responsible for the nail-scarred hands.
But for this reason there is hope for man and woman
and for this reason man and woman know "God is love."

God's gift to woman is not man.
God's gift to woman is Jesus.
So take Jesus by the hand.
Jesus is God's gift to us.

Amen

The Perfect Place

Where is everything done with ease?
In the perfect place.
Where does everyone live in peace?
In the perfect place.
Where is everyone sober and sunny?
In the perfect place.
Where is everyone as sweet as honey?
In the perfect place.
Where is there no prejudice to race?
In the perfect place.
Where is there no evil, sin, or Satan?
In the perfect place.
Where is there no love of money?
In the perfect place.
Where is there love and obedience?
In the perfect place.
And where is the perfect place?
The perfect place is in Heaven.
Amen.

Halo, Aloha, Ahoy, Howdy Doody, Hey There, Hawaii

You are a paradise on earth.
You fill my heart full of mirth
and I have dreamed of you from near my birth.

You are a work of art.
You are a desire of my heart
and I have dreamed of you from near my start.

From early in my childhood I said I would live in you.
You beautiful tropical islands with your skies of blue,
and now I do still hope to live in you, and this is true.

My cousin laughed at me when I spoke of thee.
He thought I was crazy, but we shall see.
In thee I will be but not for eternity.

For to be with God I do hope to be for eternity.
That is the Father, Son, and Holy Spirit you see.
For they are the Ones who are solely responsible
for all the good that has ever happened to me and ye.

We are forgiven in the name
of the Father, Son, and Holy Ghost.
For they are the three names
that for all of us do mean the most.

They love us you know
and they do love us so.
The vineyard God did hoe
and the seed Jesus did sow.

They are what life is worth living and dying for.
They give hope to killers, thieves, and whores.
These and others are the ones Jesus did die for.

There is still time for us to change
and this includes a big sinful range
He can cure all from AIDS to mange.

We can obey his Word or not you see.
He gives to us our free choice of how to be.
For me I choose to be like him and in he and thee.

I dream of tropical sunsets.
For very pretty ones you bet.
I hope for a life in tropical isles
where folks are happy and smile.

I dream of many a sunrise
with Wanda my sunshine.
I hope for a many a good love-in.
With Wanda it will be good lovin.

I dream of walks on the beach
with Wanda my love and peach.
I hope for many a moonlight night.
With Wanda it would be just right.

We will walk in the twilight,
which is just before moonlight.
We will let our lights shine
and serve Jesus all the time.

Walks in the morning.
Walks in the evening.
Walks with you
and Jesus, too.

Hand in hand,
walking in the sand,
beneath the bright sunshine
and beneath the bright moonshine.

Somewhere out there,
there's a place for us.
Make room out there.
Make a space for us.

So we will see you soon,
before very many moons,
and I hope you make room
for us and from us to thee,

Hawaii.

$\mathcal{A}$ Dream Come True

In a dream he was mean to me
and I mean he was mean to me.
Yes, it seems he was mean in a dream to me.
Yet in that same dream, Jesus made a dream come true
    for me.

He told me that I should say a prophecy.
The prophecy is very vague to me
but I really remember that he
did make a prophet of me.

How long will it take to finish these books?
I now remember my prophecy of 3 books.
Will there be more books?
I hope for no more books.

I ain't a saint yet.
I will be, you bet.
I now do prophesy this
and seal it with a kiss.

Nothing is what I was.
Something is what I will be.
I am not what I was.
No thanks to Satan you see.

Satan is just a drag.
I am his punching bag.
He beats me up,
he beats me down.

Satan pulled me down,
Satan made me frown.
Jesus pulled me up.
With him we'll sup.

Jesus is the One for me.
He is the Way
that I do hope to be
one day.

My lost soul he did retrieve.
I hope me he does receive.
On Jesus Christ you all must believe.
"The whole world Satan did deceive."

Yes, Satan was evil in a dream to me.
Satan was meaner than mean in a dream to me.
But Jesus was kinder than kind in that same dream to me,
Yes, no one was ever more kind in that same dream to
    me than he.

He is perfect in every way.
He is perfect both night and day.
He is the truth, the life, and the way.
He is the one and only way to be you all see,
and he is the only way to God for you and for me.

I'm so weak
but he's so strong.
He helps me to carry on.
In my heart he did put a song
and he made me feel like I belonged.

He is stronger than steel.
He has nerves of steel.
He has an iron will.
He cures the ill
without pills.

I love you
and I'm glad to say it.
I love you
and I can't make it
without you.

I love you,
and I'm gonna make a day of it
with you,
and I can't take another day of it
without you.

Yes, indeed it is true
he is a dream come true,
and he can love and bless you,
and he will see and help you through,
and Jesus will turn your gray skies to blue.

By his wisdom and foresight
we will be all right.
By his power and his might
we will be all right.
Yes, Jesus is really all right.

Amen

$\mathcal{H}$e Is in a League of His Own

On your mark, get ready, get set,
Jesus will help you over the net.

On the cross Jesus did groan.
"He is in a league of his own."

Jesus died at about 30, love.
He is as peaceful as a dove.

He knows the score.
It was us he died for.

He knows his role
and is in for a goal.

Jesus came to serve.
Praise he deserves.

Jesus will never throw you a curve.
Your admiration he does deserve.

He is God's Number One Son.
He is better than a hole in one.

Jesus is far better than par.
He is a bright shining star.

Jesus, he was hunted
and he never punted.

Jesus, he can be a holy terror
and he never makes an error.

Jesus, he can play it safe
and he gives us our faith.

Jesus, he plays not dirty pool
and he abides by all the rules.

He is strong with a will of iron
and "he rules with a rod of iron."

He is a fisher of men
and "he knew no sin."

He cannot be pinned
and he never sinned.

He cannot ever be beat
and he is a win streak.

He is brave and bold
and he gets the gold.

He gets the checkered flag
and he does not ever nag.

He does not run amuck
and he is no hockey puck.

"He is able to draw all men near"
and he can make the deaf to hear.

He can make all the blind to see.
He has good stuff for you and me.

He is on the ball.
He makes the call.

He makes the right moves
and Jesus is in the groove.

Christ is tough.
He has good stuff.

He had kind eyes all right.
He is a bull's-eye all right.

He is a Shining Knight.
He will treat you right.

He was crowned King
and he is King of kings.

He is an ace,
win or place.

He ran the good race
and he did set the pace.

He does stand his ground
and does not putt around.

He always keeps his date
and with him you can skate.

When life seems to be uphill
with Jesus it will be downhill.

He climbed the mountain of life
and Jesus is the fountain of life.

He is what life is all about
and he has never been out.

If you need something to live for,
then Jesus he will even the score.

If you are out of bounds,
then you he will astound.

If you are behind the eight ball,
then Jesus will give you his all.

If you are just treading water,
then turn to Jesus you oughta.

It is no secret what he can do
but he can still surprise you.

How much can he be?
Jesus is in for three.

He is simply Heaven.
He is over for seven.

He is no has been.
He is a perfect ten.

He is no trainee.
He is a trainer.

Jesus is no rookie.
He played no hooky.

He is never foul or out of line.
He hears protests all the time.

He touches all the bases lickety-split.
With you, he will always make a hit.

He can play hardball or softball.
His game is always with you all.

Always obey what he has to say
and you will always get to play.

Amen

Obey What Jesus Had to Say

Do you all obey
what Jesus had to say?
You must obey,
let Jesus have his way.

Jesus did say
to "love one another."
It is the way
to treat your brother.

Love is a wonderful thing.
It is better than gold or a diamond ring.
Love is what we all need.
It is something of which we should heed.

Don't you be afraid to love.
Love will come back to you.
Love the one you do think of
with a love that is oh so true.

Don't you be blue.
Jesus he loves you.
He is right for you.
Jesus is for you, too.

Do you feel bad?
Are you real bad?
Then go to Jesus.
He is there for us.

Do get high on Jesus.
He does care for us.
Get down with Jesus.
He takes care of us.

Do get right.
Try with all your might.
Do not fight.
and Jesus will be in sight.

Do hope and pray
for Jesus to stay.
Don't you disobey
or Jesus you'll pay.

Do trust and obey,
for there's no other way
to be happy in Jesus,
as The Bible does tell us.

Amen

Do Obey and Don't Stray

Do Obey.
Don't stray.
It is the way.

Do be kind.
You will find
peace of mind.

Mind over matter.
Mind Jesus Christ.
Mind your business.

No monkey business.
No clowning around.
No horsing around.

No playing around.
No pushing around.
No hanging around.

No messing around.
No getting around.
No fooling around.

Don't be a fool.
Always be cool.
Obey the rules.

Don't give up
Don't give in.
Don't put out.

Don't put on.
Don't carry on.
"Time marches on."

No time to kill.
No time for thrills.
Time to do Jesus's will.

Do what is right.
Don't be a sight.
Live not by night.

Live by day
it's the way
to be okay.

Live in the spirit.
Pray in the spirit.
Walk in the spirit.

Obey
or pay
someday.

Amen.

Obey Jesus Christ and Live a Good Life

Obey Jesus Christ and live a good life.
Obey your husband and be a good wife.
You cannot live like there is no tomorrow
or you will live a life that is full of sorrow.

Life can be good or bad,
you can be happy or sad.
It is all up to you and it is
according to how you do.

Life can be worth living,
so please don't give up.
Jesus can be gracious and giving
and then with him you all can sup.

Life can be a bowl of cherries
or life can be poison berries.
Without Jesus helping you through life,
then you will never make it through life.

If you make it through life and make one dear Friend,
then you are doing as good as you should.
If you make it through life and make Jesus your Friend,
then you will make it into the brotherhood.

If you would like the good life,
then you must learn not to want.
If you would like to go to Heaven,
then you must not sin and don't want.

If you do sin and want,
then Jesus won't
take a shine to you.
You will be blue.

If you are blue,
Jesus loves you.
You must do right
in God and his sight.

We need to
adhere to
you. Jesus
please us.

He said so.
I know so.
I ought to know.
He did say so.

Here we go.
I say do go.
We don't know
what he knows.

He knows what he is saying.
Just all of you do be obeying.
Obey his demand
and his command.

If Jesus ever does command you,
then you do as he does say to do.
You have a choice to obey his voice.
Do and be glad or don't and be sad.

It is expedient
to be obedient.
Obey what they say.
Obey them every day.

"All creation grows through suffering."
We become obedient through suffering.
"Jesus learned obedience by his suffering."
"Jesus became perfect from his suffering."

Obedience is the essence
of perfect love.
Obedience is the essence
God dreams of.

"Happy are ye when ye suffer for righteousness sake."
"Happy are ye and ye the Lord Jesus will not forsake."
"He who has suffered in the flesh has ceased from sin."
Let your heart and mind be at ease and peace from sin.

"Behold, sin no more, lest a worst thing come unto thee."
God, Jesus, and the Holy Ghost do pardon and forgive
    thee.
Try not to sin see
or you'll be like me.

If I had my life to live over again,
I would live the Christian life when
I was a young child and I was not wild.
I would be peaceful, gentle, tender, and mild.

Amen

I Would if I Could

An angel told me,
"Satan set a trap for me."
I was not worried nor did I care
and I said, "Satan should not be there."

I was a stranger
to impending danger.
Satan was my enemy.
his weapon was blasphemy.

I would like to forget I had existed.
I wish to God, Satan I had resisted.
Because then Satan attacked me
and he got me to blaspheme, see.

Satan did get me
to cuss Holy, can't you see.
I hope God kept me
innocent of cussing you see.

I hope he used a devil
to render me innocent.
If God did use a devil,
that'd be magnificent.

I hope his trap
backfires on him.
I will be glad when God shuts his trap
and when it is the lake of fire for him.

I hope it is no lake of fire for me.
I say this in all honesty.
I hope he has better plans for me
when I repent, you see.

Jesus, do be patient
with me thy patient.
I hope I will be free from sin again
and I do hope that my sin will end.

Jesus is my probation officer.
Jesus is always in his office.
I can check in at any time
and he tells me I am fine.

What is this thing called grace?
That gives us time to find face.
Grace is love
and God is love.

In the first place,
I will be glad when I sin no more.
I'm under his grace
and this is what Christ came for.

I am under his grace
until I get to a place
where I no longer sin
and I am free again.

I may not sin
until the end.
It is hard to win
and overcome sin.

It is hard to shake
bad sinful habits.
He can make us shake
the bad sinful habits.

I would not dare sin if you were around.
I would not go there if you were around.
I would not hate but love.
I would not lust over busts.

I would stop smoking.
I would stop joking.
I would stop fussing.
I would stop cussing.

Now let it be understood,
I don't do as I should.
I would do good,
if I only could.

I would be right and not wrong.
I would be strong and belong.
I would be aware and beware.
I would be careful and care.

I would not be a clown,
if I could calm down.
I would not lust,
if I could just

get it under control
and have you to hold.
I would if you were here.
I could if you were near.

I would like to be in control of myself.
I care not to be in control of any else.
I belong by myself,
away from all else.

It is easy to forget yourself.
It is hard to forget yourself.
Gain control
of your soul.

This is easier said than done.
But Jesus Christ is the one
who can help you gain control
and make your soul whole.

Jesus do make us whole
and bring us back into the fold.
Jesus please free we the oppressed;
for we are distressed and we are depressed.

There are so many of us
Jesus,
who need to be set free
by ye.

Any time
is fine
with me
ye see.

Maybe Jesus will set me free.
Maybe God will deliver me
from every evil work
and that evil jerk.

Maybe he will set me free,
free to be as I should be.
Please do set me free,
it is all up to thee.

Maybe someday I will be free.
I hope so you see.
Maybe someday I will be well,
only time will tell.

I wish I was well
and not in this hell.
All is not well
in this here hell.

Something has to give.
Somebody has to give
for me to be well
and out of this hell.

I am downtrodden
and plowed under.
I have hit rock bottom
and been put asunder.

I have hit rock bottom
many a time.
I look forward to Autumn
and a love of mine.

I have gone about as far as I can go,
I will have you know.
Please no more for me,
not for me.

I have gone about as far as I can go.
I have gone about as far as I will go.
I will have you to know,
I am tired of this show.

I have carried it
all I care to carry it.
I have been a dope.
Life has been a bad soap.

There is no good soap.
They give us no hope.
Life is bad,
I have had.

I am barely treading water.
God keeps me afloat.
I do not do like I oughta.
God gives me hope.

I am drowning in sorrow.
I hope for no tomorrow.
I am over my head,
I wish I was dead.

Jesus, please rescue us;
for we are drowning see.
God, please deliver us
and we will praise thee.

I have not come this far
without a heap of help.
I wear Satan's scar.
Jesus, he did help.

Jesus, look down upon we poor fools,
who do not obey all of your rules
and lend us a helping hand
and help us make a stand.

Amen

The Rod of Correction

An angel told me, "I was in trouble."
I needed help on the double
but I busted her bubble.

I was a schlep.
I said, "I need no help."
But I was beat by God to a whelp.

He beat me with a rod of correction,
to give my life a new direction
and be under his protection.

Father is stern for our own good.
God turned me over to Satan so I would
grow up and learn how to be, as we all should.

I needed to grow up and learn how to be
and to be punished for the way I had been you see.
So this is why God The Father he did decide to beat me.

My mind and heart and body was filled with torment
and I got down on my hands and knees and did lament.
So I did grow up and I did pay my debt in full payment.

My life is much better now.
I did grow up and how.
To God I now bow.

I would not forgive others, don't you see.
So God, Jesus, and Holy would not forgive me
until my debt of sin was fully paid, don't you see.

Now my debt is paid and they do forgive me
and now I am no longer tormented, you all see.
My torment was not brief but it is a relief, you see.

Satan and his were the tormentors of me
and they really did give it to me.
They nearly destroyed me.

He really gave me a hard time.
He nearly destroyed my mind.
God, Jesus, and Holy were kind
and they did restore my mind.

Satan, he did make me suffer
but it turned me against him.
I grew because I did suffer
and now I do love God Elohim.

If Satan had left me alone,
I probably would not have made it home.
All that he did was wrong.
If I get to see him burn, I may sing a song.

"Ding dong the devil's dead. Harold
Which old devil, the evil devil. Arlen
Ding dong the evil devil's dead."
This song I may sing to that devil.

Satan is a ding dong.
Satan is Mr. Wrong.
He is not Mr. Right.
He will burn all right.

He might put up a resistance
and fight for his existence.
He might put up a fight.
It will be quite a sight.

He is the most evil Devil
who respects no age level.
Young, middle-aged, and old,
his heart toward all of us is cold.

Go away.
Take a hike.
Get lost.
and drop dead.

Satan is smart like a fox.
Don't get put in his box.
Enough now you have taken.
"Get thee behind me, Satan."

Don't look back,
Satan may be gaining on you.
Satan may attack
the body, heart, and brain of you.

The brain is a delicate thing.
It feels pain and feels strain.
The heart is a good work of art.
It plays a part from the start.

Satan tormented my heart
from a very early start.
Satan tormented my brain
til I was nearly insane.

Satan tried to drive me insane with oh so it goes
but Satan is crazy and not sane, so here it goes.
Among other things, he did run it through my head
to try to drive me crazy so I would kill myself dead.

He tried to put me in his hotel, an insane asylum.
He tried to put me in there in this past millennium.
However, God had different plans for me and him,
to remain sane, and fix this book, and bruise him.

It is hard to remain sane
when Satan torments my brain.
He tried to drive me crazy.
He made my muddled mind hazy.

He worked on me with anxiety and depression.
I must admit he did make an impression.
He made me schizophrenic,
until I was demonic.

Satan worked on me with sleep deprivation
among other things as my insanity initiation.
Satan tried to drive me insane with lust
but I do now know he is not one to trust.

You cannot trust Satan or anyone,
only God and Jesus Christ his Son.
"The spirit is willing but the flesh is weak,"
only God and Jesus Christ his Son ye seek.

I hear a loud and annoying ringing in my left ear, which
    I gave to Satan.
I hear a soft and soothing ringing in my right ear, which
    I gave to Jesus.
It is hard to hear the ringing in my right ear
because of the loud ringing in my other ear.

But I am aware that Jesus is there
and that he for me does still care.
Don't give Satan anything
but give Jesus everything.

Give him your temple.
Give him your dimple.
Give him your soul.
Give him it whole.

Give him your mind.
Give him your time.
Give him your heart
and you will not smart.

"You have to give the devil his due?"
Give Satan nothing.
The devil is soon to get his due.
He is nothing.

Do not give in to Satan or sin
or heaven you may not get in.
Beware of Satan sneaking up behind.
To be like Jesus is a dream of mine.

Hold on tight to your dreams,
no matter how bad it seems.
God will give you your heart's desires,
if with Satan you never ever conspire.

"Trust in the Lord."
"Delight thyself also in the Lord;
and he shall give thee the desires of thine heart."
God knows who is for you and he can get you a sweetheart.

To be like Jesus is a dream of mine,
to be like Jesus throughout all time.
Jesus is a Friend of mine,
I will love him for all time.

Amen

To Be Like Jesus
Is the Way to Be

I had an out-of-the-body experience you see.
An angel showed me Satan messing with me.
I told her, "He is not hurting me," you see.
And she had nothing more to do with me.

Satan was all over me,
trying to destroy me.
He would have succeeded
but Jesus, he interceded.

I did not care what happened to me
and I did not care about my soul.
I did not care at all you see
and this I have told.

I told Jesus and Satan to compete for my soul.
And this is where this story begins to unfold.
Satan tried everything in his power to destroy me
but Jesus would not let him destroy me you see.

Jesus won the battle for my soul
and he did make me well and whole.
And now that this story has been told,
I will be glad when I am back in the fold.

If I ever do get back in
I'll never go out again.
I have had enough see,
no more for me ye see.

Jesus did make me free from sin
but I was soon in bondage again.
It is now up to me to be sin free.
I must overcome Satan to be

the way I am suppose to be.
To be like Jesus is the way to be.
And this is a tall order for you and me.
But I think that we can do it, don't you see.

I did rebel.
I was headed for hell.
He was nailed.
This was hell and swell.

Jesus is great and swell.
Jesus went through hell
for ye
and me.

He died for ye and me.
Jesus deserves to be
King of kings,
Lord of lords.

He took it for me,
don't you see.
He did die for me
and set me free.

Jesus gave up his life for me
so that I might live for eternity.
I owe God, Jesus, and Holy everything.
I owe that damned evil devil nothing.

Jesus is helping me.
God is making me
what I should be
for eternity.

God in me is doing a good work.
God delivers us from evil works.
This is what I read.
This is what it said.

God has delivered me
from every evil work.
God please shine on me
and burn that evil jerk.

"God hath delivered us from the power of darkness,
and hath translated us into the kingdom of his dear Son."
"The Lord shall deliver me from every evil work,
and will preserve me unto his heavenly kingdom:
to whom be glory for ever and ever."
"Thine is the kingdom, and the power,
and the glory for ever and for ever."

Amen

Our Boss Was on the Cross

"Seek ye first the kingdom of God, and his righteousness, and all things shall be added unto you."
"The kingdom of God is not meat and drink; but righteousness and peace and joy in the Holy Ghost."

"Peace on earth good will toward men."
God did send his love for to save men.

"God is a rewarder of them that diligently seek him."
"Seek God." "Seek ye me, and ye shall live."

"Let us count the ways that we love thee." Elizabeth Browning

"We love God, because he first loved us."

"For God sent not his Son into the world to condemn the world;
but that the world through him might be saved."
"For God so loved the world that he gave his only begotten Son,
that whosoever believeth in him should not perish, but have everlasting life."

"Whosoever believeth in the Son of God should not
perish, but have everlasting life."
"Whosoever believeth in the Son of man should not
perish, but have eternal life."

"The Lord is not slack concerning his promise, as some
men count slackness;
but is longsuffering to usward, not willing that any
should perish,
but that all should come to repentance."

Actors can act
but do they know how to be?
Are they fact
or making lies on stage and TV?

"To be or not to be, that is the question?" Shakespeare
"To be like Jesus Christ is the answer." God Jehovah

There is only one way to be,
out of the two ways to be you see.
There is the wrong way or Satan's way.
There is the right way or Jesus Christ's way.

The way to be is like Jesus you see.
That is the way to be for you and me.
The Christian way is the way to be.
That is what life is all about, Alphie.

"I have set before thee this day life and good and death
    and evil."
"Depart from evil, and do good; seek peace, and pursue it."

"Turn a deaf ear to evil."
"Love good and hate evil."

The only God is Good.
And only God is Good.

"God is good to the evil."
"God is kind to mankind."

"Peace on earth, good will toward men." "Live in peace."
"Mark the perfect man; for the end of that man is peace."

One has to be perfect
to correct the imperfect.

"No one is perfect?"
Some Christians are perfect.

I am soon to be a perfect Christian.
I am no longer a primitive creature.

I am soon to be a teacher-preacher.

I now do know just how to be
And I am soon to be sin free.

He paid for all our sin
but not time and again.

I was a servant of sin
time after time again.

"You have to stand for something or you will fall for
    anything."
I did stand for nothing and I did fall for just about
    everything.

"Stand not in the way of a sinner."
You may die and not be a winner.

You may make it worse
and make them adverse.

"One sinner can destroy much good."
Turn it over to Jesus as you should.

"Being made free from sin, ye become servants of
    righteousness."
"Stand fast therefore in the liberty wherewith Christ
    hath made
you free and be not entangled again in the yoke of
    bondage."

Life can be hell.
Jail can be hell.

If everyone was behind bars
who ought to be behind bars,
then all would be behind bars.

"Two prisoners were in jail. One saw the bars and one
saw the stars."
"Let freedom ring, let freedom ring, raise your hands and
dance and sing."

Jesus Christ can make you free
and jail is not a fun place to be.
Jesus can make the captives free
and Jesus Christ does it for free.

"You cannot buy love?"
Jesus bought my love.

"You get what you pay for.?
Our sins Jesus did pay for.

I am not mine.
I am not Satan's.
I am Jesus Christ's,
paid for with a price.

"You don't get something for nothing?""Salvation is free."
"You may be a slave of sin.""The truth will make you free."
"You will be free indeed, if Jesus Christ makes you free."

"Nothing lasts for ever?"
"For we shall for ever be with the Lord,"
and we shall be free as a bird in a tree."

How many people have died in the name of freedom?
When Jesus Christ, he died in the name of freedom.

The body is fragile
but it is practical.
I hate this shell
that endures hell.

Our bodies were created on earth.
Our souls were created in heaven.

"Fear not them which kill the body but are not able to
   kill the soul."
"Fear him which is able to destroy both soul and body
   in hell."

"We have nothing to fear but fear itself?" Winston
   Churchill
"We have nothing to fear but God himself." Jesus Christ.

Jesus said, "Fear God."
God said, "Fear Jesus."

"Where angels do fear to tread?"
Angels are obedient and fear not.

"Fear not, little flock;"
"for God hath not given us the spirit of fear;
but of power and of love $and of a sound mind."

"There is no fear in love;
but perfect love casteth out fear.
He that feareth is not made perfect in love."

Perfect is how to be,
when we are made free.

Perfection is our goal,
when we are made whole.

"Behave thyself wisely in a perfect way."
"Thou shalt be perfect with the Lord thy God."
"Be ye therefore perfect, even as your Father which is in
    heaven is perfect."

"Be ye holy; for I am holy."
"I am the Lord your God."

"Thou shalt have no other gods before me: for I the Lord
    thy God am a jealous God."

Billy Graham said communism would fall because 90
    percent of the people believe in God.

"The fool hath said in his heart, There is no God."

"For those who do believe in God, no explanation is
   necessary."
"For those who do not believe in God, no explanation
   is possible."

"All things are possible with God."
"Nothing is impossible with God."

Just speak the word
or think the thought
is all God has to do
and it will come true.

"All things are possible with God."
God is there for me and for you all.

"Be still and know that God is God" for real.
"Be for real" and live life with great zeal.
Live life and "be ye doers of good will"
and live without the crutch of a pill.

"There is no hope with dope."
Christ can help you to cope.

"Drug free is the way to be."
I do tell you this honestly.

"Honesty is the best policy."

Alcoholism is not a disease.
Alcoholism causes disease.

There is something to "rye whiskey, rye whiskey, I'll drink
    till I die."
There is no reason why you should drink till you die. Live
    in Christ.
The bartender was absolutely right when he said "Name
    your poison."
"When does an alcoholic become an alcoholic? With the
    first drink."

"Drink a little wine for your infirmities."
Be not a worker of evil or iniquities

Drinking does affect your thinking.
Start thinking instead of drinking.
Stop drinking without blinking.

"No drunkard shall enter the kingdom of God."
"Come alive and thrive with Jesus and then God."
"No effeminate shall enter the Kingdom of God."
Come alive and thrive with Jesus and then God.

Say no to sin,
again and again.

"Be gentle and kind."
"Be of sober mind."

"Be of good cheer."
"No booze or beer."

Be no boozer.
Be no loser.

Be no sinner.
Be a winner.

I was a boozer.
I was a loser.
I will soon be a winner
when I'm not a sinner.

Do dip no snuff.
That is enough.

Don't toke
or smoke.

You may think that smoking is fun and cool and there
   ain't nothing like it.
But I say that smoking is not fun, you fool and there ain't
   nothing to it.

Smoking carcinogen is a sin.

Chewing tobacco is awful,
down to every awful jawful.

Don't chew.
It won't do.
Do and be blue.
It is a sin, too.

Smoking, snuff, and chew
may be the death of you.

Drugs make you not care.
Drink makes you not care.
Life can make you not care.
Death makes you not care.

"Don't get high
and OD and die."

DUI
DOA
LSD
DOA

From pothead
to deadhead.

Life or death.
Take no meth.

No smack.
No crack.
No crank.
No prank.

Get with it.
Get a grip.
Get a hold of yourself.
Get control of yourself.

No drugs,
only hugs.
Don't do dope or drugs,
only holy kisses and hugs.

Don't take crack.
Don't look back.

Look forward to Jesus,
the one who pleases us.

Stop today.
Don't delay.

"Good medicine is good."
Do take it as you should.

Smoking, drinking, and drugs are hard sinful habits
    to brake.
Ask Jesus Christ to help and set you free for heaven's sake.

Drugs and alcohol do affect the heart and brain.
Drugs and alcohol do make you do sinful things.

They make you swear
and make you not care

Satan can do the same
but so are we to blame.

The devil made me do it?
There is no excuse to it.
The devil made me do it.
It's likely the devil did it.

It is what you need that counts.
What you want does not count.

No need for greed, no need to hoard; for there is enough
  to feed all.
No need for worry, now need to fret; for he is not through
  yet.
No need for strife, no need to fight; for he is right.

Do not fight,
it's not right.
Jesus will fight for ye.
Jesus is right for thee.

Jesus prefers we be meek
and we turn the other cheek.

"Be not a striker." "Be meek" and "turn the other cheek."
"Be slow to anger." "Let not the sun set on you anger."
"Be angry but sin not" and "forsake not the assembly."
"Be not conformed to this world." Do overcome the world.
"Be not biminded." "Be cool and be of modest apparel."
Be mild, gentle, and loving, and don't be a wild child.

Be not like me. Please be not like me.
"Be not a liar." "Be not deceitful." "Be not contrary."
"Be not wicked." "Be not an evil doer." "Work not iniquity."
Be not a glutton for food, work, punishment, pain or
    anything.
Be not crazy. "Be not lazy. Consider the ant thou sluggard."
Be sane. Be safe. Be sure. Be secure. Be pure.
Be not unclean. you know what I mean.

I am not interested in guys,
especially not in gay guys.

No more oral sex.
No more anal sex.

No more sodomy.
No more lottery.

Do not hook up.
But do look up.

Be satisfied with her paps. Do be cool and don't be saps.
"Be satisfied with your wages" and "don't strike or sue."
"Be content with your earnings" and "don't fuss or cuss."
"Neither a borrower nor a lender be." Be a cheerful giver.

"Owe no man."
"Hate no man."
"Salute no man."

"There is a time appointed for every man to die but after
     this the judgment."
"The Father judgeth no man, but hath committed all
     judgment unto the Son."

No one ever got away with anything at anytime.
Jesus sits in judgment and judges all the time.

His judgments are true
and he does judge you.

Jesus is sweet
but he rules with a rod of iron.
Jesus is neat
and he cares of this soul of mine.

"God is not a respecter of persons."
Be you not a respecter of persons.

The supreme court
is the Devil's court.

You do repent.
Do not repeat.

Don't be bad, belligerent, bizarre, berserk, or a jerk.
Don't make fun of anyone or it could happen to you.
Don't act tough, don't be rough, bluff, and no hot stuff.
Don't talk, text, twit, or tweet, except when necessary.
Don't hang out, and don't freak out, and don't strike out.

Don't put off, and don't goof off, and don't scratch off.
Don't eat, drink, talk, or talk on the cellphone and drive.
Don't drive on ice, go slow on snow, and take drivers ed.
Don't follow to close or you may wreck and be the first
    there.
Don't exceed the speed, you should take heed indeed.

Slow down and live longer.
Calm down and be stronger.

God can settle you down.
He won't weigh you down.

Get back,
sit back,
settle down
and get down.

Do slow down
and get there
safe and sound.
Show you care.

Slow down,
shut down,
cool down,
calm down.
Trim down.
Slim down.

Mess up?
Fess up,
make up,
rest up.

Tighten up,
loosen up,
hang tight,
hang loose.

Keep going,
keep rowing.

Don't give up,
no matter what.

So good,
so far.
Do good,
you star.

Opportunity knocks.
Jesus Christ rocks.
Be saved
and behave.

Wake up before it's too late
or you will have an ill fate.

If you do not grow up and behave,
you are headed for an early grave.

Grave robbing has to cease.
Let the dead rest in peace.

"Let the dead bury the dead."
You should live life instead.

You can live the good life.
You can have a good wife.

There is everything good for you.
There is nothing you cannot do.

"I can do all things through Christ which strengthens me,"
even though it may seem insurmountable or an impossibility.

I can honestly win.
I can overcome sin.
I can overcome evil.
I can overcome Satan
and overcome the world.

"Whatsoever is born of God overcometh the world."
"To him that overcometh will I give to eat of the tree
    of life,
which is in the midst of the paradise of God."
"He that overcometh shall inherit all things;
and he shall be my son, and I will be his God."
"Who is he that overcometh the world,
but he that believeth that Jesus is the Son of God."

If I had more strength,
I honestly think
that I could overcome
and a son become.

"Love not the world, neither the things that are in the
    world."

"People don't fall off the world because of gravity."
"People don't fall off the world because it sucks."

Of the world beware,
it's a jungle out there.

The world is not a safe place to be.
My refuge is Jesus and God Almighty.

Red, yellow, white, brown, black, and blue
might will not do but God Almighty can do.

"Red, yellow, black, and white,
all are precious in God's sight."

We were created for his pleasure
and we are all for God's treasure.

Creation was not created with a big bang
but she will be destroyed with a big bang.

I am surprised the world has lasted this long
with everything about the world that is wrong.

"God will create a new heaven and earth,
wherein dwelleth righteousness
and there will be no sea."
"Heaven and earth will have a new birth,
wherein dwelleth righteousness"
for all of you and for me.

God created the universe.
God created animals for us.

"The chicken or the egg, which came first?"
God the Creator created the chicken first.

"Our ancestor is not a monkey."
"Our ancestor is God Almighty."

God is Almighty.
God is Alknowing.
God is Allpowerful.
God is Omnipotent.

Do not overestimate you yourself.
Do not underestimate God himself.

God is God I AM.
We just barely is.
Jesus is God I AM's.
And we all are his.

"Ye belong to Jesus and Jesus belongs to God."
"He is our intercessor and mediator with God."

Pray today,
don't delay.
Pray tonight
and pray right.

He pays attention to our prayers and needs.
He pays back the guilty and criminals indeed.
"Crime does not pay."
No one ever got away.

He paid the price for our sins and crimes.
Jesus is "a Friend" that "loveth at all times."

"What a Friend we have in Jesus." Joseph M. Scriven
"What a Friend and More Christ is." Our God Jehovah

"Dog is man's best friend?"
"Diamonds are a girl's best friend."
God, Jesus, and Holy are our best Friends.

Cows are not holy.
Smoke is not holy.
Toledo is not holy.

The Holy Spirit is Holy.
"The law is good and holy,
And "the commandment holy,"

"Jesus said, "I came not to change the law
but to fulfill the law
and hang all the sayings of the prophets on the law."

"Holy, holy, holy is the Lord of hosts."

"Greet ye one another with a holy kiss."

Be ye tender to one another.
Be ye loving to one another.
Be ye caring to one another.

"Be ye of one mind and for ever be kind."
"Be ye of one spirit and sing spiritual songs."
"Be ye not high spirited as is a wild horse."
"Be ye down to earth and as gentle as a lamb."

"Birds of a feather flock together."
I say to thee, we are much better.

Vegetarians, you can eat meat
but watch what meat you eat.

It is all right to eat some animals.
It is not all right to eat all animals.

"God made some animals for meat."
Don't you worry about what you eat.

"You are what you eat?"
"You are what you are."

Are you a sinner or a saint?
You can't be both, you can't.
There ain't no way, there ain't.

"The good die young?"
"Only God is Good."

"Man shall not live by bread alone, but by every word that
    proceedeth out of the mouth of God."
"Whosoever shall do the will of God, the same is my
    brother, and my sister, and my mother."

Obey God's will all your life.
Do take charge of your life.
Do put a charge in your life.
Don't charge away your life.

"He that loveth his life shall lose it."
"He that hateth his life in this world shall keep it unto
    life eternal."
"Whosoever shall save his life shall lose it."
"Whosoever shall lose his life for Christ's sake shall
    find it."

Be a winner, not a loser.
"You have nothing to lose
and everything to be gained."
It is entirely up to you to do.
Nothing but success will do.

"Treat others as you would have them treat you"
and treat your pets with love and kindness, too.
You can pet your pets on the head
and see that your pets are well fed.

News for zoos, don't give your animals the blues.
Treat your animals well and don't give them hell.

No treating animals harshly.
No beating animals severely.

No experimenting with animals.
No abusing animals rights.

No fishing with dynamite.
No killing deer by night.

No rooster or dog fights.

No dogs left at home alone.
No cats left at home alone.

No goldfish in small bowls.
No canaries in small cages.

No bird brain ideas.
No lame brain ideas.

No veal.
Be real.

"God has tens of thousands of angels."
"God has 20,000 chariots of fire,"
"drawn by horses of fire."

"Let your light shine."
Don't be a behind.

"Don't be a disgrace
to the human race."

Don't cry crocodile tears.
Don't cry from all the jeers.
Don't cry over monster fears.

It is a sad thing to mistreat or abuse an animal.
Some animals have sex and some people have sex.
Those couples that God hath joined together make love.

"Thy shalt not commit adultery."
Be committed to your marriage.

"First comes marriage and then comes the baby carriage."
"Fornication is the only reason for divorce from marriage."

"Man and woman must be of equal yoke."
You must have the same belief for hope.

"Blessed is the man whose God is his hope."
God is there for man at the end of his rope.

"God resists the proud,"
and I do detest the loud.

Don't boast.
Don't roast.

Do be true.
Do be true blue.

Do not act.
Do not act up.

Don't act big, for ever be humble you must.
Don't be little and don't lust over a big bust.

"Don't tell little white lies."
"Don't tell a whale of a tale."

"Don't lie with a dog."
"Don't lie like a dog."

Don't be a liar
or you will not hear yourself screaming
for the roar of the fire.

Don't be deceitful
or you may speak through false teeth
for having a forked tongue.

"An unbridled tongue is as evil thing."
"Do, see, hear, and speak no evil thing."

Do say what you mean and do mean what you say.
Watch what you see on T V and watch what you say.
Don't say what you think but think about what you say.

"Sticks and stones may break your bones
but bad words they may break your heart."

Satan has ruined every language with cuss words.
"God will give us a pure language" with new words.

I do murder the English language.
"God will give us a pure language."

Clam up.
Shut up.
Hush up.
Grow up.

The gift of gab?
Talk just a dab.

"Let your yea be yea
and your nay be nay."

Be of few words.
Be of God's word.

"God is not mocked."
Keep thy lips locked.

"Thou shalt not take the name of the Lord thy God
    in vain;
for the Lord will not hold him guiltless that taketh his
    name in vain."

Jesus Christ† said, "It is not what goes in the mouth
that defiles but that which comes out of the mouth."

"Aaron's wife said something about Moses marrying
    an Ethiopian,
so God gave her leprosy for seven days."

"The serpent was underhanded with Eve,
so God took his legs out from under him."

"It is a fearful thing to fall into the hands of the living
    God."

"God is not the God of the dead, but of the living."

Somebody said God is dead.
I did not know God was sick.
God is neither sick nor dead.
God cares about the sin sick.

"Vengeance is mine saith the Lord."
"Repentance is mine saith the Lord's."

I hear too much about punishment and justice
and not enough about forgiveness and mercy.

If you will not forgive others,
then God will not forgive you.

"All have sinned and fallen short of the glory of God."
I would not forgive others, so I was punished by God.

"We are to forgive one another seven times seventy."
"Blessed are the merciful for they shall obtain mercy."

"Bless your enemies."
"Love your enemies."

No more an eye for an eye.
No more a tooth for a tooth.

"When you point your finger at someone, there are three
    of your own fingers pointing back at you."
"Judge not, that ye be not judged. For what measure ye
    mete, it shall be measured" back to you."

"Take the beam out of your own eye,"
"before the mote out of another's eye."

"Whosoever shall lead into captivity
shall themselves go into captivity."

"The truth will make you free."
"Mercy and truth be with thee."

"Tell the truth, the whole truth, and nothing but the
    truth so help me God."
"Glory, glory, hallelujah, his truth goes marching on."
    George F. Post
"Onward Christian soldiers marching off to war, Text
    Sabine
with the Cross of Jesus going on before." Boring-Gould

"Love God," "Love one another," and "Love thy neighbor."
"Thou shalt not bear false witness against thy neighbor."

Fairy tales and fables are false.
God is the one who is true blue.

"Thy word is true from the beginning."
God's Word Jesus was the beginning.

God's word is meant to be obeyed always
and Jesus Christ obeyed them always.
Jesus's word you can count on always.
He said, "Lo, I am with you always,
even unto the end of the world."

"Heaven and earth shall pass away
but God's word shall not pass away."
They are the same today and always.

"The pen is mightier than the sword."
Don't sin and always obey God's word.
"He who takes up the sword,
shall perish by the sword."

There is just no humane way to kill a person.
The humane way is to have mercy on a person.

A terrorist
is terrible.

Meaning well
and doing well
are two different things
and mean different things.

Get rid of your gun.
Get rid of every one.
Get rid of your knife.
Please keep your wife.

Satan is a killer
and a wheeler dealer.

Jehovah never told anyone to kill.
The Bible says, "Thy shalt not kill."

"Thy shalt not kill."
"Thy shalt not steal."
Do it and pay you will.
Commandments are real.

"God says what he means
and God means what he says."
God please save us by all means
and God has no mean streak, we say.

Do not be mean.
Do not be a scream.

Do not be cruel.
Do not be a fool.

Do not be woolly.
Do not be a bully.

Do not tease.
Do say please.

Do say thank you.
Do say welcome.

Do be kind
and do mind.

"Faith, hope, and charity,
the greatest of these is charity."
"Charity covers a multitude of sins."
Charity means kindness, time and again.

If we do obey their every command,
then we shall always be in demand.

We will obey
all they say.
We must I say,
trust and obey.

Take care
and do care.

There is a lot to say about Jesus.
He does live to take care of us.
Throw all your cares to him.
He will talk to God Elohim.

Men, women, and children, pray to Jesus.
Sons and daughters of God, pray to God.
Pray to your Father, who art in heaven.
Pray for all of us to make it to heaven.

Heaven will be our haven.
Jesus will be our leaven.

Somewhere
out there,
there is a place for us
with God and Jesus.

"Jesus had something negative to say about praying in
    public."
"Jesus had something positive to say about praying in
    private."

Pray for the living and not for the dead.
"Pray not for death," pray for life instead.

"Jesus holds the keys to death and hell."
He sits in judgment and he judges well.

Hell is for real.
Hell hurts a great deal.
Brimstone smells.
All is not well in hell.

"Hell is in the center of the earth."
"Earth is the center of the universe."

"From hell, to hello, to halo."

Now know that trick or treat is obsolete.
Instead of trick or treat on Halloween,
how about "treat me sweet on Can Day."
Yes this is what you all ought to say.

Instead of never mind,
how about always mind.

You should not mind children if they mind you and do
as you say do.

"Satan is at work in children of disobedience."
Children obey your parents and be expedient.
"Honor thy mother and father" and be obedient.

Ye youngies beware,
Satan is out there.
He can get your soul
and dig you a hole.

Little children, they abide and endure.
But they need your help, it's for sure.

Don't be a juvenile delinquent
or you may be in hell frequent.

If you do beat them with a rod of wood
and you beat them for their own good,
then they will grow up as they should.

If you do "spare the rod and spoil the child,"
in all probability, they will grow up to be wild.

I grew up to be a monster and I was wild.
Please do not let this happen to any child.

There is yet hope for me,
thanks to God Almighty.

If tall trees could talk, I imagine the would say, "Grow up."
Grow up before your past God Almighty he does throw up.

"The children of the kingdom shall be cast out into
    outer darkness:
there shall be weeping and gnashing of teeth."

Grow up or it's out you go.
Don't be childish you know.

No more childish acts.
No more molestation acts.
No more perverse acts.
No more degenerate acts.
No more dirty talking.
No more dirty dancing.
No sexotic dancing.
No sextravaganza.
No sextramarital.
No sexhibition.
No sexcapade.
No sexercise.

Don't moon.
Don't spoon.

Don't fork.
Don't abort.

Sexercise makes babies.
Please no more babies.

Please adopt a child.

A child is impressionable.
Adults are impressionable.

Children can be cruel.
and adults can be cruel.

Children are children.
Children are not kids.

"I believe that life begins before conception,
and children are in your care the their protection,
and children are entrusted unto you for their direction."
Please make your children ready for Jehovah's inspection.

"He who provides not for his own is worse than an infidel."
So take care of your children and care for them well.
Bring them up the right way or they will give you hell.

"Show and tell children well."

"Honour thy father and thy mother."
"Love your sister and your brother."

"Children obey your father and mother or it's death to
    pay."
"Children of disobedience do die at an extremely early
    age."

Fathers and mothers "provoke not your children to wrath."
A child becomes a man or a woman at twelve years of age.

"There is no excuse for child abuse."
If you have children, you will study
The King James version of The Bible
and learn how to be with children.
"Who has more children than God?"

Teach your children yes and no
and teach them in the way to go.

Teach your children never ever to sin,
so they will not have an untimely end.

Teach your children about the world,
so they will be wise boys and girls.

Teach your children about "the birds and the bees."
Give them a wise understanding of nature please.

Teach your children to know right from wrong,
so to the Lord Jesus Christ, they will belong.

Teach your children who is the boss.
All should know who is the boss.
Our Boss was on the Cross.

The war was won on the cross.
The battle still rages on.
Jesus was our boss on the cross.
On him you must lean on.

Lean on Jesus.
Jesus lean on.

Not my will be done
but thy will be done.
Not our will be done
but thy wills be done.
Jehovah's will be done
and Jesus's will be done.

"Lean not unto thine own understanding;
for God's ways are higher than our ways."
"God can give thee peace that passeth all understanding."
Servants, "take the word to the highways and the byways."

For Jesus there was no death bed,
no place to rest his dying head.

Satan killed Jesus.
The Jews killed Jesus.
The Gentiles killed Jesus.
We all live because of Jesus.

If you don't know Jesus, then you are at a loss.
He is the One who paid the cost for the lost.
If you are at a loss, then go to Jesus who knows.
He and his Father are the Ones running this show.
If you have any questions, then go to Jesus.
He has the answers and may give them to us.

If you are an atheist, then may God help you.
If you are an agnostic, then God is for real.
If you are in a gang, then please get out.
If you are gay, then there is a better way.
If you are astray, then you know the way.

If you make it to heaven, you may get "a crown of glory
which fadeth not away."
If you make it to heaven, you may get "a new name of
which no man will know."
If you make it to heaven, you may get "to see Satan burn
in the lake of fire."
If you make it to heaven, you may get "to see all of your
loved ones again."

"Blessed are the poor in spirit: for theirs is the kingdom
of heaven."
"Blessed be ye poor: for yours is the kingdom of God."
"A rich man shall hardly enter into the kingdom of
heaven."

"It is easier for a camel to go through the eye of a needle,
than for a rich man to enter into the kingdom of God."

I say tax the rich people.
Make them homeless people.

They that did not help the poor,
give all their money to the poor.

Jesus may make us poor
so we may become rich.

Money, give it away,
don't throw it away.

"God loves a cheerful giver."
Give more than just a sliver.

"It is more blessed to give than to receive."
Give and be blessed beyond what you believe.

"Give and it shall be given unto you."
"Give and God will really bless you."

God gave us oil to use.
Use it and don't abuse it.
Be careful and be shareful.

Show that you care
and give and share.

Please give to the poor
from your heart's core.

"God hath chosen the poor of this world rich in faith,
and heirs of the kingdom which he hath promised to
    them that love him."
"Thou shalt love the Lord thy God with all thine heart,
    and with all thy soul, and with all thy might."
Love God and Jesus and the Holt Spirit and always and
    for ever do what is right in God's sight.

"God seeks those who worship him in spirit and truth."

"All have sinned and fallen short of the glory of God."
Praise and glory to Jesus and praise and glory to God.

Praise God in the highest.
God is God of the highest.

My God what a heart.
God is set apart.
God is kind and smart.
God is holy and art.
My God what a brain.
God remembers everything.

"God is all knowing."
God's mind keeps on going.

If I am here next year,
I hope for more cheers,
and I hope for less tears.

The world is as cold as ice
and she is paying the price.

If it would stop the vice,
maybe it would be nice.

The world is bad
and it is getting worse.
It is very sad
and it needs a nurse.

Away from this sick world,
to the place we would all love to be.
Away from this sick world,
to home sweet home for you and me.

Away from this sinful world,
to the way, the truth, and the light.
Yes, it's up, up, and away from this that's right.
We may fly up high in the sky and we may be
"changed in the twinkling of an eye,"
and there will be no good-byes.

Up to heaven and away from this world.
Up to heaven and true love, boys and girls.
Up to heaven and we will be gone in a whirl.

"What goes up must come down?"
Up to heaven and not come down.

But until that time, we all must stay in line.
We must not waste time and walk the line.

Don't you worry, there is no hurry.
Do take your time and do stay in line.
Older people can help us stay in line.
They can be helpful and have the time.
Jesus keeps them safe and they do mind.

"Older people are our national treasure."
They are experienced, wise, and our elders.

You should say yes sir and no sir to anyone older than you.
You should say yes ma'am and no ma'am to the elders
    of you.

Instead of yes sir,
how about yes sire.

Obey what they say or it's death to pay.
"Trust and obey for there's no other way."

Young, middle-aged, and old,
"be cool" and don't be cold.

No more cold wars.
No more hot wars.

I am against this man's army.
I am for the Salvation Army.

"War is horrifying
and not glorifying."

"War is hell."
War is a sin.

War is a waste,
a waste of lives,
a waste of resources
and a waste of money.

Fighting
and dying
for what,
it's nuts.

Eat or be eaten.
Kill or be killed.
What a world
boys and girls.

My love has waxed cold.
Down unto my very soul.

I am a Christian
and not a politician.

Christianity first. Democracy last.

The separation of church and state.
I do say do away with the state.

I do say do away with the military.
You are evil if you say the contrary.

Do away with the electoral vote
and establish the popular vote.

Do away with the two-party system
and establish the one-party system.

The American party
should be the party.

"A house divided against itself cannot stand."
The house and the senate should be 1 band.

The senate delete.
The house delete.

They should be wise Americans
who serve the king of America.

Our national anthem is God Bless America.
And it is up to us to be the best of America.

Our nation America is in bad trouble.
She had better change on the double.

Our nation America she does need an upheaval.
"The love of money is the root of all sorts of evil."

America needs a revival,
in order for her survival.

America would be dead today,
if not for Christ's graceful way.

America puts people to death.
She is taking her last breath.

America has never won at war.
She is never ever to go to war.

America has gone astray.
She is going her own way.

America is sin sick
from getting kicks.

All should watch how you get your kicks.
All the way from veteran to draft picks.

"You get so much to do so little."
"Bodily exercise profiteth little."
"The flesh profiteth nothing."

"Use it or lose it."
Abuse it and lose it.

America, wake up and shape up
and do start playing heads up.

Every day
except Sunday
can be our playday.

"The Sabbath was made for man and not man for the
    Sabbath."
Play not on the Sabbath and do what is good on the
    Sabbath.
Work not on the Sabbath and do not eat out on the
    Sabbath.

"Remember The Sabbath day to keep it Holy."
On The Sabbath think of God, Jesus, and Holy.

"Thy shalt make no graven image."
Do away with your graven images.

"Thy shalt not covet."
The Bible, I do love it.

I love thee.
I love thou.

Do not waste your power away
that God Almighty gave ya.
Save it for resurrection day
or it will backfire on ya.

"Waste not. Want not."

"The Lord is my shepherd, I shall not want."
Be OK having what you need and don't want.

You will be all right always my friend,
if you get what you need my friend,
rather than what you want my friend.

Satan gives us what we want for a price
and what Satan does take will not be nice.
Before you deal, you had better think twice
or for you there will be no wedding with rice.

Take not the mark of the beast
or you may miss the wedding feast.

"Mark not the body" and worship Jesus.
Get down to the bare essentials with Jesus.
"Having food and raiment let us be content."

Get rid of the sin in your life and repent.
There is still time for you all to change.
It is your present you must rearrange.

There is still time for your life to count.
It is your future life that really counts.

There is no future in horoscope signs.
Our goal is to be with Jesus divine.

There is no future without Jesus you see.
Our goal is to be with Jesus for eternity.

There is no sin in Jesus you see.
Come on, the way to be is sin free.

"The wages of sin is death."
Come on and don't take meth.

There is no such thing as Mother Nature.
Come on, it's according to God's pleasure.

The Lord is in control of the weather.
Come on ya'll, let's all get it together.

It is time we all must unite as one.
That's the way that it is simply done.

If you all must, cry. But you all must try.
"Just trust and obey, for there's no other way."
And just don't you ask why, just you trust and try.

If with Satan you all do converse,
then he may make you adverse,
and you may do the reverse,
and you may be subverse.
And when he is through
putting you all through
a thorough thrashing,
your only thought
will be naught
or nothing,
insanity.

Or maybe he will not cut you any slack.
Perhaps he will put a monkey on your back
and your body, brain, and heart he will attack,
with torture, torment, pain, and make you insane.

"An idle mind is the devil's workshop."
Stay busy, from president to carhop.

Work by day,
not by night.
It's the way
to live right.

Work is good.
Play is good.
They are good for me,
when I have the energy.

You must try and work extremely hard and don't be lazy.
You must try to resist him or he will try to drive you crazy.

Satan you must resist.
You must try and persist.
With Christ you could coexist.
It is a matter of which God insists.
Jesus is searching for soldiers to enlist.

If he does choose you, then do what is right.
You must obey his word and walk in his light.

You must always hope and pray because
you cannot stay out of "harms way" because
"Satan is going to and fro devouring who he may."
You can study The Bible and learn what you should say.

If Satan does make a deal with you, then it will cost you
    your very own soul.
"What does it profit a man if he gain the whole world
    and lose his own soul."

Body and soul,
be made whole.

Mind and heart,
be kind and smart.

That Satan was dumb.
God's heart went numb.

Satan said in his heart, "I will ascend to the north
and put my throne above God's." Heaven is north.

Satan sinned from his start,
right from his jealous heart.

Satan is called devil
because Satan is evil.

Jealousy is bad news.
It gives us the blues.
Especially for me,
don't you agree?

He was jealous of God
and he wanted to be God.

He said he alone was perfect
so he made others imperfect.

He was fairest of fair,
yet still not all there.

He was brutally handsome,
now Satan he is just brutal.

There is a lot that Satan did not think about.
He will have a lot of time not to think about
what he has done
to most everyone.

Satan is going to pay for what he did to everyone.
Satan is going to pay for harming each and everyone.

Pay he will
in the hot kill.

He added insult to injury.
He added insult to perjury.

He beat me down
and he beat me up.

You can take the bad Satan can give
because of the good the Lord can give.
You can take the worst Satan can give
because of the best the Lord can give.

He did his worst to me.
He got the best of me.
Satan was bad for me.
Jesus was good to me.

Hope for the best
and look out for the worst.
God is the Best
and Satan is the worst.

"Jesus resisted the temptation of the devil."
"Jesus shall destroy the works of the devil."

"Greater is he who is in you, than he who is in the world."
"He paid the price for you. Not only for you but the world."

"If God be for you, who can be against you?"
"If God be against you, who can be for you?"

Jesus means helper.
He is God's helper.
He is our helper.

Do your best and hope for the best.
Jesus will help you over the crest.

Though your troubles seem to come in twos.
Jesus will help see you through your blues.
We all do look to Jesus to see us through
all that that evil Satan might try to us to do.

Jesus the Christ had this advice for all of us to do.
"Do unto others as you would have them do unto you."

"Do not forget but please remember
the Lord's birthday is in December."

"On Easter morning as the sun does rise
think of how Jesus the Christ he did rise."

When I hear hammering, I think of all
Christ went through for me and you all.
Christ is The Greatest Blood Donor all.
He gave all his blood for all Christians.

Think of what all he went through;
for all of us and for all of you, too.
It has boggled the mind
throughout all AD time.

Short and tall,
great and small,
he loves us all,
and he walks tall.

It is as simple
as ABC and
as one, two, three.
The trinity they do love thee
and Jesus Christ is for me and ye.

As sure as he met ya,
he is going to get ya.
on that you can bet ya.

There is no such thing as luck
and don't you worship the buck.

If you all like to gamble,
you don't stand a chance.
Unless you choose Christ,
then you all are born to lose.

If you are lost in sin and you cannot win,
hope and pray for Jesus to take you in.

"You win some. You lose some.
You tie some. Some are rained out."
Be a winner with the winner Jesus Christ

"He that denieth that Jesus is the Christ is a liar."
"He is Antichrist, that denieth the Father and Son."
"Every spirit that confesseth that Jesus Christ is come in
    the flesh is of God."
"Every spirit that confesseth not that Jesus Christ is come
    in the flesh is not of God:"
"and this is that spirit of Antichrist, whereof ye have
    heard that it should come."
"Little children, it is the last time: and as ye have heard
    that Antichrist shall come,
even now are there many Antichrists; whereby we know
    that it is the last time."
"Beware of false Christs."
"Beware of false prophets."
"Beware of evil workers."
"Beware of concision."
"Beware of Satan."
"Beware of dogs."
"Beware of men."

"Surely I come quickly.""Amen. Even so, come, Lord Jesus.
The grace of our Lord Jesus Christ be with you all. Amen."

I Will Be Glad

I will be glad when grace is over
and when we are rolling in clover.

I will be glad when we are home at last,
now enough I have had of my bad past.

I will be glad when we are home at last
and when we have learned from our past.

I will be glad when we do not suffer anymore,
when we are grown-up and don't sin anymore.

I will be glad when it is through
and there are nary more blues.

I will be glad when it is done
and there is nary more hon..

I will be glad when it is finally final.
I will be glad when it is the finale.

I will be glad when it is complete
and when we can all take a seat.

I will be glad when it is at an end
and there is nothing left to tend.

I will be glad when it is finished
and all the work is replenished.

I will be glad when there is nothing left to do
and we can all see the eternal light of all you

from everlasting
unto everlasting.

Amen.

I See the Light

"He who sows the whirlwind."
"He will reap the whirlwind."

God said, "Let there be light."
"And there was light."
"God saw this was good" all right,
and God he was right.

I will wait and see
just how it will be.
If he will be for me
or will be agin me.

I sinned a great deal.
I did pay a great deal.
I was damned if I do
and damned if I don't.

I was sick of being sick.
I was tired of being tired.
I was tired of being lied to.
I was tired of taking hits, too.

I was bored and I was a bore
and I had nothing to live for.
Everything I did was wrong
and nothing I did was right.

I was stressed out
and I was fed up.
I did give up.
He said hup.

I'll have you know,
I'm ready to say no.
I've gone about as far as I can go.
I'm tired of being in this ole show.

It has been tough.
I had had enough.
I have taken about all I can take.
New friends I do need to make.

I need some Christian friends,
new friends until the very end.
I had taken just about all I could take.
I was at the point that I would brake.

I wanted just to die and to be no more.
That was the best that I could hope for.
I was ready to die if my life did not change.
My life needed to change and be rearranged.

I would have died of being lonely,
if it had not been for Jesus only.
I lashed out at God and Jesus when I was down.
I hated everyone and wished they were not around.

Sometimes I wished Jesus would go away and let me alone.
Sometimes I wished Jesus would go away and just go
home.
I am glad he did not.
I do owe Jesus a lot.

Jesus is the only way to be.
Satan will burn for eternity.
Jesus is our example.
Satan is our insample.

Jesus made me feel glad.
Satan made me feel sad.
Jesus made me feel rad.
Satan made me feel bad.

Satan and his were bad for me.
Jesus and his were good to me.
Satan and his were mean to me.
Jesus and his were keen to me.

Satan and his were ice to me.
Jesus and his were nice to me.
Satan was wrong to me.
Jesus was right for me.

Satan gave me hell.
Jesus made me well.
For me no more hell.
For us this is swell.

Now this I do tell.
I do wish you well.
I do wish that all I had ever done
was stolen a piece of bubblegum.

I have learned my lessons the hard way in the school
of life.
And now I do look forward to God, Jesus, Holy, and a
new life.

Jesus did help me
and now I do see.
I do now see the light.
I am ready to do right.

Amen.

I Am Ready

Ever since my young birth,
for me, it has been hell on earth.
Satan has influenced my life until now.
I am ready for my life to change and how.

I am ready for the desires of my heart.
I think this is a good place to start.
I am ready for Wanda, my true love.
She is the one that I do dream of.

I am ready for a home in Hawaii
where folks there say, "How are ye?"
I am ready for a car the color of my eyes.
I think that this would be no big surprise.

I am ready for a more abundant life.
I am ready to be as sharp as a knife.
I am ready for a good and loving wife.
I am ready for the end of my life and strife.

I am ready to be born of the spirit
and to be baptized with the spirit.
I am ready for a heavenly body
and to dwell in heaven's lobby.

I am ready for a lot of light
so my eyes will shine bright.
I am ready to be full of light
and to have power and might.

I am ready for the Holy Spirit.
I am ready to be a holy angel.
I have studied God's Holy Word.
I am ready to meet a Holy God.

I am ready to belong to Holy God and Jesus
and to sing praises unto them in the chorus.
And last but not least
is the wedding feast.

If God does have his own way,
I won't lust over a bust.
If God does have his own way,
I won't fuss and or cuss.

If God does have his own way,
I won't smoke anymore.
If God does have his own way,
I won't want anymore.

If God does have his own way,
I won't die soon.
If God does have his own way,
I will live soon.

God's will be done,
both Father and Son.
God's will be done,
by Jesus his Son.

Now that I am God's son,
I ask Father's will be done.
I ask Father for these things.
I ask Father in Jesus's name.

I ask for a lot
but I need a lot.
I might not get them in this life
but I hope I get them in this life.

I may not get it.
I may just get it.
Will I get life
or get death?

Are we near the end
of my bad life of sin?
I will have to wait and see
what God has in store see.

I am ready for more.
Is there more in store?
I am ready for life more abundantly.
I am ready for a wife to comfort me.

I am ready for a change in my life.
I am ready for to rearrange my life.
I am ready to stop smoking for them.
This would be a good token to them.

I am ready to repent.
I am tired of doing my stint.
I am ready to do right.
I hope I put up a good fight.

I am ready to stop sinning.
I am ready to start winning.
I am ready to obey,
all they have to say.

I am ready to say how high up,
when they tell me to jump.
We will jump when they say hup,
when we are over the hump.

I am ready for life to go my way
and I hope that my way is ye way.
Have your way
is what I do say.

Thy will be done
O, Father and Son.
I am ready to be more than I am.
Please hear me Great God I AM.

I am not sure what I am.
I wish I knew what I am.
Am I a star from afar
or am I a brat or a rat.?

I am not sure what I am.
I am not brave whatever I am.
Am I man or am I mouse.
I hate to go out of the house.

I am not sure what I am.
I am not much whatever I am.
Am I man or son of I AM?
It is a mystery to me you see.

I am not sure what I am.
I hope I am spirit whatever I am.
Am I flesh or am I spirit?
I hope I am borned of the spirit.

"God seeks those who worship him in spirit and truth."
Am I flesh or spirit? I just do not really know.
I just do not really exactly know which is the truth.
I love who he is and what he is, this I do know.

I remember that I was questioned about God.
And I said, "Praise God" very weakly inside.
Then I said, "I said praise God weakly inside."
And an angel said, "That's the spirit and truth."

I am ready for the truth.
I do truly need no proof
that Jesus is Lord
and "Lord of lords."

I am ready to die for my faith in Jesus Christ.
This is the only reason worth losing your life.
I am ready to live if the Lord gives me my heart's desires.
But if God does not, then I hope that my death transpires.

I have accepted death.
I am ready for death.
I am waiting on death,
contemplating death.

I wish I was finished so I can die.I
I do not care to live anymore.
I am fed up with life and ready to die.
I do wish for death and no more.

Life has got me down.
I wish I was not around.
No more life for me,
I am ready to die, see.

I am ready to die.
I wish I would die.
Life is just a bore,
nothing to live for.

I am ready to die
and I don't care why.
My life can end now
and I don't care how.

I am ready to die,
right now I do cry.
If this does carry any weight,
I am ready to meet my fate.

I am ready to die.
I just want to die.
I do not want to suffer anymore.
I want to die and to be no more.

I am ready to die.
and if you wonder why.
I have suffered, my oh my.
I do need a good reason to try.

I am ready to die
but I had very much rather live.
This is truly no lie.
In Jesus name I ask God to give.

I am ready to die, and to be taken up high in the sky,
and to "be changed in the twinkling of an eye" with no
    good-byes.
Mortality shall put on immortality and we will be
    immortal.
"Corruption shall put on incorruption" and we will be
    incorruptible.

I did come into this world alone.
I may go out of this world alone.
I did come into this world with nothing
and I will leave this world with nothing.

There is nothing to hold me here.
I do hold nothing at all dear here.
There is nothing at all,
Jesus, please end it all.

There is no reason for me to live
and I do have nothing left to give.
I am sick of it all.
Please end it all.

I am sick of this old world,
this world makes me sick.
There is nothing here
that interests me here.

I do hate my life in this world.
I have lost interest in this old world.
No wine, women, or song boys and girls.

I am ready to leave this old world.
There is nothing for me in this world.
I am ready to go to heaven, boys and girls.

Amen.

Life a Living Hell

The world will be better off without me.
That is the way that I do think it will be.

I will be gone very soon,
before very many moons.

After I am shot dead in the head,
then I will be gone as I have said.

Life to me is just not at all worth living anymore.
I do not care anything about anything anymore.

I can do without it,
no doubt about it

Life sucks don't you see.
I am stuck in a rut see.

Life is just a bitch.
Bury me in a ditch.

Life has been hell
alone in this well.

Life is hell.
Life smells.

I do think
life stinks.

Stop and smell the roses,
Smell 'em with your noses.

Right now I look forward to death,
for it shall mean a brand-new life.

Maybe my life will change for the better
before we are in heaven and are together.

If my present life does change, I can stop my sin.
I would like to start over with a sin-free life again.

Again I smoke, lust, and cuss.
I must overcome I just must.

I may smoke, lust, and cuss to the end.
What a damned hell of a life it has been.

Life has been a living hell for me,
right up until now, don't you see.

Life has not been all a waste,
thanks to God's good grace.

Life has not been good,
not been as it should.

Life has been bad.
Life has been sad.

Life has been a bad dream.
Life has been a big scream.

Life has been horrible.
Life has been terrible.

Life has been misery.
Life has been agony.

Life has been rough.
Life has been tough.

Life has been bust.
Life has been lust.

Life has been awful.
Life has been sinful.

Life has been sin,
time & time again.

I am ready to begin
a life free from sin.

A life free from sin,
up until my very end.

Give me death.
No more breath.

Or give me a good life
and give me a good wife.

Life is a rat race.
Life is a fast pace.

Life isn't always what you make it.
Satan is around to brake and take it.

My life could be much worse and it really has been.
My life could be much better and I do hope it will be.

Perhaps if I had a better life,
then maybe I could live right.

I look to God, Jesus, and Holy for life more abundant.
I hope this is not getting to sound boring and redundant.

I will be soon again sin free.
I will be soon perfect ye see.

My sins will be soon before you.
Please don't ever do as I did do.

Do not and do live.
Do and you may die.

I forgive everyone who has harmed me.
I hope those I have harmed forgive me.

We must us all look to Jesus,
who never harmed any of us.

Look to the One who is true
and he shall see you through.

Listen for the shout, it shall be loud.
Look for him returning in the clouds. Amen.

Life after Death

No need to cry,
you may not die.
But for those who do,
there is hope for you.

You would not be so blue,
if you knew what was in store for you.
There will be peace of mind
where there will always be Son shine.

There will be plenty of time
to read and write and rhyme.
There will be loved ones you know
and there will the love flow, you know.

There will be no wars.
There will be no bores.
There will be no fights.
There will we do right.

Maybe we will get to see Satan burn
because he simply would not learn.
Maybe we will get to hear him scream
because he was such a bad dream.

Maybe God will give us
a tour of God's universe.
Maybe we will get to see our star
close up and not from so very far.

We will praise our God night and day.
We will obey all that God has to say.
We will serve our God night and day.
We will have peace of mind I do say.

We will see God.
We will love God.
God will love us,
and so will Jesus.

Holy will love us, too,
me and you.
We will always be happy,
you and me.

Happy for eternity,
is how it will be.
Happy for eternity,
for you and me.

Amen.

The End and Life Again

It might be the end
but there is life again.
It is not the end of life
but the beginning of life.

Life anew,
out of the zoo.
Life anew
for me and you.

Life eternal.
Life with God.
Life with Jesus.
And life with Holy.

No more sin.
No more Satan.
We shall win
and not be taken.

No more hell.
No more cells.
You can tell,
It will be swell.

No more wars.
No more chores.
No more death.
No last breath.

No more worry.
No more hurry.
No more pain.
No more rain.

No more hate.
No more rape.
No more killing.
No more stealing.

No more sorrow.
No need to borrow.
No singing the blues.
No bad but good news.

No more greed.
No mouths to feed.
No more money
but milk and honey.

No more slackness
but much wealth.
No more sickness
but good health.

No more heartaches.
No more backaches.
No more insanity
toward humanity.

Vios con dios.
Adios amigos.
Until we meet again
my very good friends.

Bye de bye,
by and by
and tallyho
off we go.

Good-bye, old world,
I hope I do outgrow you.
Good-bye, cold world,
it's been bad to know you.

There is nothing of this world
worth living and dying for boys and girls.
The war and battle against sin
still rages on for all of us men and women.

"Fight the good fight"
and do what is right.
We must overcome
this world and "run

the good race."
Set the pace.
Don't lose face
and win the race.

Win for God.
Win for Jesus.
Win for Holy.
Win yourself.

Be a winner.
Be no sinner.
Do repent.
Don't relent.

This is pretty good stuff,
if I may say so myself.
I cannot get enough
of God, who else?

This book is good,
if I do say so myself.
For us it is good
and for everyone else.

I am ready to put this in a computer
and become a Christian tutor.
The next book will not be in rhyme
but about my life and a hard time.

"Blessed is he who has a good life."
"Blessed is he who has a good wife."
"Bless people who have not."
"Bless people and curse not."

I am ready to be blessed.
Please be my guests.
I am ready to be assessed.
Please no more tests.

I am tired of being cursed.
I need to be nursed.
I am tired of being damned.
Please no more I AM.

I am getting tired.
I do need to stop.
I do not wanna get fired.
I do like this work a lot.

I am tired from lack of rest,
most of the time.
I am not ever at my best
in body or mind.

I must rest now.
I am tired now.
I am tired of it,
be back in a bit.

It is Sunday.
I will rest today.
I am tired from yesterday.
I will not do much work today.

It is a Sunday,
the Sabbath day.
It is a rest day,
a Hallowed day.

I am glad today
is Sunday,
the Sabbath day,
the rest day.

I need to rest,
I am suppose to rest
on this day,
the Sabbath Sunday.

I will get plenty of rest today
anyway.
It is the Sabbath Sunday
I say.

I'll rest today,
it is a Sunday.
I will not work today.
I will not play today.

I will rest today.
It is a rest day.
I look forward to our rest day,
when we do no work or play.

No way
today.
There is no way,
I'll work today.

It is good I don't have to work today.
I am unable to work anyway.
I am too tuckered out.
I will chill out.

I need to,
I have to
lay down
and rest up.

I must lay down and rest
so I will be at my best.
I confess,
it is best.

I will rest.
It is best
Shall I rest?
I shall rest.

I will rest
and digest
what God has said
and what I have read.

I have the rest
of the day
to rest
I say.

It is time
to unwind
my mind.
Do be kind

to me
ye see
and I will be
kind to ye.

I am too tired to go on.
I wish that I was home.
Please strengthen me,
so I can finish you see.

I just woke up around 1:30 a.m.
I am ready for work God I AM.
God put me to work
so I will not be a jerk.

Right now I do not feel like giving up.
Right now I do not feel like resting up.
Hut, two, three, four,
give me some more.

I wish you would give me all of it
so I will be done with it.
Please give me the rest
so I can rest.

God, I like it when you put ideas into my head.
It is pretty clear what to do when you do.
I like it as I have just said,
please do.

If there is anymore,
please give it to me
because I am bored
and rested you see.

Come alive
and thrive.
Do keep your head,
until you are dead.

If I was dead
as I have said.
I could not serve Jesus.
So what is left for all us.

I was a nincompoop
for wishing I was dead.
I was thrown for a loop
by what Satan did and said.

I was a lame brain
for wishing I was dead.
I was totally insane.
I was crazy in the head.

I was a knucklehead
for wishing I was dead.
I was a birdbrain
for my raising Cain.

I was a nitwit head
for wishing I was dead.
I now hope for a life
that is free from strife.

Now it is my number one wish.
Father, do please grant me this.
Please make me happy,
so I won't be so crabby.

Father, please make me happy
and put an end to my misery.
Father, please make me glad.
I am tired of being very sad.

Father, please give
and do let me live.
Let me live a good life
and get me a good wife.

Father God, please give me more
and give me something to live for.
I need something besides cigarettes.
I need a reason to live for you do bet.

I do ask these things
in Jesus Christ's name.
I do ask them of you
and I hope you will do

them for me.
I do honestly
need some help.
Please God help.

I need a helpmake.
I need a helpmate.
I need a soul mate.
I need a playmate.

I do need to be whole Mate.
Please make me whole Mate.
Please do it once again
and free my soul from sin.

Do make us well,
so that we can tell
how Great Thou Art,
Greater than Walmart.

Please make me well
and save me from hell
so that I can tell
how good and swell

thou art to us.
Father, we love you
and we do love Jesus,
and we do love Holy, too.

I do hope that I am through
and there is nothing else to do.
Father and Jesus, we do love you
and Holy Spirit, we do love you, too.

Thank you, God,
for a job well done.
Thank you, God,
for Jesus, your Son.

Thank you, Jesus,
for dying for us.
Thank you, Jesus,
for living for us.

Thank you, Holy,
for healing our hearts.
Thank you, Holy,
for a brand-new start.

God, Jesus, and Holy have kept me going through all
 these years.
They have seen me through all my heartaches and all
 my tears.
Maybe they will see me through to my end.
Maybe it will be a whole lot better until then.

Maybe tomorrow
will be an okay day,
with less sorrow
than today, I do pray.

God, Jesus, and Holy,
they look after me.
They cared for me
and they care for me.

They do not pamper me.
They do not hamper me.
I have free will
to do their will.

It is God's will that we not sin.
It is Satan's will that we do sin.
Are we doing God's will?
Are we doing Satan's will?

My will
is to do God's will
until I die.
In Jesus's name I will die.

This time
maybe I will die.
It is fine,
I'll no longer sigh.

No need to fear,
my time is near.
I have too much time
and not enough time.

It does appear
my time is near
without you near
without you dear.

I am getting to close to my end
to mess up again.
My life has been a life of sin,
I am near my end.

Dying is easy,
living is hard.
It can be breezy
out in the yard.

Life can be rough.
You must be tough.
I am battle weary
but no longer teary.

I am a casualty of war
but now stronger than before.
I am aware of Satan's wily ways
and I will grow stronger in my last days.

Suffering I have come to expect.
Suffering I have come to accept.
It is through suffering that we know.
It is through suffering that we grow.

The world has some growing up to do.
And I have some growing up to do, too.
Let us grow.
Let us know.

Woman must learn
and man must learn.
You have a lot to learn
in a short time to learn.

We have a long way to go
and a short while to get there.
It is time to get ready to go,
we will smile when we get there.

We live this life,
the school of life
to learn how to be
in the next life, see.

I have lived through the school of hard knocks.
And I have learned that God is not mocked.
I have learned more,
much, much more.

I have learned how not to be
and I have learned how to be.
I have learned right from wrong.
I have learned wrong from right.

Live and learn.
Live and yearn
for God's righteousness,
for your righteousness.

Live and learn.
Learn or burn.
It is how you all do.
It is all up to you.

I thought I was through many times.
I have been blue many times.
I have learned "it is not over
until it is all over." Yogi Berra

I hope you are wiser now
and will be good and how.
What a trip this has been.
This is Amen and The End.

$\mathcal{A}$ God-Given Gift

"Every good gift and every perfect gift is from above, and cometh down from the Father of lights, with whom is no variableness, neither shadow of turning."

Scribe
Huster

Source
The Holy Bible
King James Version

God is the author, the follow-up to Amazing Grace
A vision of God's eyes, a poetic sermon